# HOLD ON!

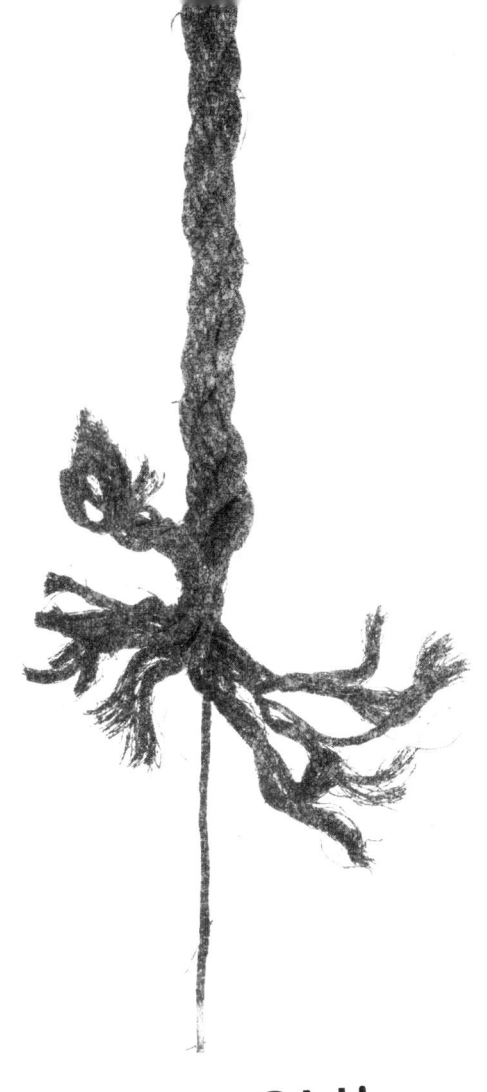

# HOLD ON!

*Surviving the Days before Moshiach*

ROY S. NEUBERGER

Copyright © 2021 by Roy S. Neuberger

ISBN: 978-1-952370-59-5

All rights reserved. No part of this book may be used or reproduced or transmitted in any form or by any means, electronic or mechanical, including photocopying, recording, or by any information storage and retrieval system, without written permission from the publisher.

Published by Mosaica Press, Inc.
www.mosaicapress.com
info@mosaicapress.com

# YESHIVA DARCHEI TORAH

YAAKOV & ILANA MELOHN CAMPUS, IN MEMORY OF REB YOSEF MELOHN, ל"ז

Rabbi Yaakov Bender
Rosh HaYeshiva

Tammuz 5779

To my dear friend and a friend of all Klal Yisroel,
Harav Reb Yisroel Neuberger, shlita:

I have had the zechus of reviewing much of what you have written in your latest sefer. I am thrilled to tell you how much it has meant to me. The scope and breadth of your knowledge is incredible.

I would urge every Jew to find the time to read all of your seforim. You are a genius of Jewish history. You are a true lamdan. You are a man with real hashkofos haTorah. Gedolei Yisroel have borne witness to your greatness, so who am I to add?

You bring out such wonderful emotions in me, about how proud I am to be a Jew. You tug at the pintele Yid in every single Jew.

May Hakodesh Boruch Hu give you the wherewithal and strength to continue your Harbotzas Torah for many happy and healthy years to come.

Yaakov Bender

Rabbi Yitzchak Berkovits
Sanhedria HaMurchevet 113/27
Jerusalem, Israel 97707
02-5813847

יצחק שמואל הלוי ברקוביץ
ראש רשת הכוללים לינת הצדק
סנהדרי"ה המורחבת 113/27
ירושלם ת"ו

בס"ד, ירושלם ת"ו ב' דר"ח אייר תשע"ג

    In a day and age where political correctness is seen as the supreme value, the time has come for someone to stand up and tell it like it is. Rabbi Yisroel Neuberger with his passion for the arrival of the Moshiach, could be accused of making some people feel uncomfortable, but every word he speaks is truth. One cannot help but remember the saintly Chofetz Chaim who posted signs in his home town of Radin pleading with the local non-Jewish population to begin observing the seven Noachide laws in anticipation of the coming of Moshiach.

    The message is important even to the most observant of Jews. Is our own relationship with The Creator, our emunah, our bitachon, and our middos up to the standards appropriate for the era of Moshiach? And perhaps, is our concern for the future of the Jewish nation geniune to the point that every one of us does what he can to share with the uninformed the authenticity and relevance of Torah values?

    I commend Reb Yisroel on his courage, passion and persistence and hope that this book will penetrate the hearts of many and hasten the coming of Moshiach.

בברכה,

יצחק ברקוביץ

## RAV SHLOMO BUSSU
### JERUSALEM

הרב שלמה בוסו
ירושלים תובב"א

Adar II 5779

בס"ד

The words of the Rambam, *z"l*, about what is destined to happen in the period when Moshiach comes, are well known (*Hilchot Melachim* 12:2). He writes that these matters were hidden from the *nevi'im*, and even the Sages did not receive a specific tradition about them. One can only attempt to gain somewhat of an understanding from the *pesukim*, "For no man will know how all these things, or what is similar to them, will emerge, until it actually happens." The Rambam's intention of writing this is clear: that presently the knowledge of these matters has no relevance to our fulfillment of the Torah and mitzvot.

Nevertheless, in this generation, the winds of heresy that are rampant, blowing in every nook and cranny, have left their stain and mark even amongst Bnei Yisrael. We have witnessed the consequences, that though Bnei Yisrael are "מַאֲמִינִים בְּנֵי מַאֲמִינִים – believers, sons of believers," they are not acting as they should. It is not uncommon that peoples' conduct contradicts all the basic principles of *emunah* and *bitachon*!

And if this is the fact regarding their daily living, how much more so with regard to their looking forward to the coming of Moshiach. They don't recognize that by doing so they are jeopardizing their merit to live and see the great and joyous redemption, which is in essence, the purpose of the Creation of this world. Our precious friend, Rav Yisrael Neuberger, *shlita*, who has been blessed by Hashem Yitbarach with an amazing talent and ability of writing and expression, and who has already gained high regard with his previous books and articles, has made a very wise choice in taking advantage of his special skill in order to bring merit to Bnei Yisrael; to awaken them from the slumber of their routine lives on the one hand, while also portraying the meaning and great significance of the *geulah*. All this through amazingly illustrating and depicting the time we so much hope will come quickly.

The clear and intended purpose of this *sefer* is to arouse and awaken one to hope for the *geulah*, and to pay careful heed so that one will have the *zechus* to be from those who will live and survive the "חֶבְלֵי מָשִׁיחַ – birth-pangs of Moshiach."

With great respect and admiration, I recommend this *sefer*, which is written with wisdom, fear, counsel and understanding. With respect of the great toil that was invested into it, and with great admiration of the long strides that has been achieved by the *rav* and author, the precious Rav Yisrael Neuberger, *shlita*, who has ascended from depths of abyss, where he hardly knew about his Jewish roots, to be transformed into one who teaches and disseminates so many vital principles of Judaism. One can tangibly feel that his words have been written with concern for *Am Yisrael*, and love for every Jew.

He needs no more than a *berachah* that his wellsprings continue pouring forth, and that he merits to continue spreading and increasing the honor of the Torah and those who learn it – with even more energy and vigor, with good health and *siyatta diShmaya*, "עַד כִּי יָבֹא שִׁילֹה וְלוֹ יִקְהַת עַמִּים – until the arrival of Shiloh, and the gathering of peoples by him," speedily, in our days, *amen*.

With the *berachah* of Torah and with great love,

*Shlomo Bussu*
Shlomo Bussu

דוד קאהן

ביהמ"ד גבול יעבץ
ברוקלין, נוא יארק

ב"ה אור לח' אדר א' תשס"ד

As I perused Reb Yisroel Newberger's "Survival Handbook" I was reminded of a bon mot from the late Gerer Rebbe Rav Avrohom Mordechai Alter זצ"ל when he saw a train and applied this experience to a Musar Hachkifo: "It's interesting to see how one hot one can pull many cold ones". Reb Yisroel exudes deep feelings of faith which can inspire multitudes. If one reads only the titles of the chapters in this book, one is moved.

I pray that Reb Yisroel go from strength to strength in his holy work to prepare Klal Yisroel to serve Hashem in order to accelerate our redemption.

החותם באהבה ויקר
דוד קאהן

# CONGREGATION KNESETH ISRAEL

**THE WHITE SHUL**
728 Empire Avenue
Far Rockaway, NY 11691
Phone: 718.327.0500
Fax: 718.327.7415
www.whiteshul.org
office@whiteshul.com

בס"ד

**Rabbi**
Rabbi Eytan Feiner

**Assistant Rabbi**
Rabbi Motti Neuburger

**Rabbi Emeritus**
Rabbi Ralph Pelcovitz זצ"ל

**President**
Domenico Antonelli

**Executive Vice President**
Heshie Lazar

**Senior Vice President**
Matis Hedvat

**Second Vice President**
Sadi Benzaquen

**Vice President, Programming**
Barry Salamon

**Vice President, Youth**
Yechiel Zlotnick

**Secretary**
Brian Nadata

**Treasurer**
Daniel Liss

**Legal Counsel**
Sidney Lipstein

**Chairman of the Board**
Chaim Dahan

**Vice Chairmen of the Board**
Nesanel Feller
Tuvia Silverstein

8 Iyar 5779
May 13, 2019

    The author of the widely acclaimed *From Central Park to Sinai* and *2020 Vision* has now penned perhaps his most important work yet. In his *Survival Handbook for the Days Before Moshiach*, my dear friend Roy S. Neuberger has done the Jewish People a great service, providing us all with a meaningful guidebook to best prepare ourselves for Moshiach's imminent arrival and eschatological times.

    Passionate, powerful, and thought-provoking, the author's latest book propels us to ponder the myriad ways we can navigate the "birth-pangs of Moshiach" and emerge unscathed and truly worthy of redemption. Mr. Neuberger begins by painting a portrait of the sordid world scene today, but proceeds to elucidate – with fervor and his typical sanguine and ever-optimistic tone – how we can survive the pervasive turmoil and illuminate our lives to the fullest degree. And enlighten the world at large in preparation for the end of days.

    Poignant and persuasive, the author's *Survival Handbook* has succeeded beautifully in conveying with candor the means through which we can flee the vices of our current society, and perfect ourselves as true servants of the Almighty. Mr. Neuberger's salubrious attitude is infectious, and the reader will depart from the compelling work feeling energized and spiritually invigorated to join this wonderful and inspiring Jew in getting ready to greet Moshiach. May he come speedily in our days, and may we merit the all-encompassing redemption we have so yearned for all these years.

With utmost respect and admiration,

Eytan Feiner
Rabbi

Member of ORTHODOX UNION

קהילת בית יהודה צבי
הרב יעקב יוסף הכהן פייטמאן

395 Oakland Avenue
Cedarhurst, NY 11516
516-374-9293
www.kbyt.org

כ"ו אייר תשע"ט
May 30, 2019

**HaRav Yaakov Feitman**
*Morah D'Asrah*
**Ari Hahn**
*President*
**Menashe Oratz**
*Vice President*
**Uri Dreifus**
*Gabbai*
**Yossi Kraus**
*Secretary*
**Michoel Greenfield**
*Treasurer*

לכבוד ידידי Reb Yisrael Neuberger נ"י :

The great leader of Agudas Yisrael, Rabbi Moshe Sherer זצ"ל who was like a second father to me and my rebbe in עבודת הכלל had a wonderful saying: " It is important to do things for Klal Yisrael, but you also must never forget Reb Yisrael." This could have been said about you, Reb Yisrael as well. In all of your works and speeches you discuss grand issues such as the "battle between Yishmoel and Esav and "*Yemos Hamoshiach*." But you also never forget about the individual Jew and his needs. Indeed, you are the ultimate "Reb Yisroel."

Your book *Survival Handbook For the Days Before Moshiach*, like its predecessors, is amazing: clear, concise, exciting and most important, rooted in Torah sources from Chumash to contemporary *Gedolim*. One of the most important components of the *Handbook* is your personal inspiring story, which is told with your usual candor, courage and sparkling insights into life.

Additionally, through wonderful graphics and the use of "boxed highlights," you present guidance for our age from giants such as the Vilna Gaon, Rav Samson Raphael Hirsch, the Chofetz Chaim and Rav Chaim Yisroel Belsky זכרונם לברכה. Although this book provides a firm groundwork of Torah sources for every idea, it is also an extremely practical work, making it a true Handbook for our time. Since this is a book about survival, several chapters give pragmatic advice on how to get to the age of Moshiach intact and both physically and spiritually healthy. I highly recommend this book to scholar and beginner alike.

With all my ברכות and אהבה ,
Rabbi Yaakov Feitman

**RABBI YAAKOV HILLEL**
Rosh Yeshivat
Hevrat Ahavat Shalom
45 Arzey Habira St. Jerusalem

יעקב משה הלל
ראש ישיבת
חברת אהבת שלום
רח' ארזי הבירה 45 ירושלים

בס"ד, כ"ח אדר ב' תשע"ט

 My dear friend R. Roy Neuberger has shown me his new *sefer*, "Survival Handbook for The Days Before Moshiach." It is based on a broad range of *pessukim*, *maamarei Hazal*, and teachings of the *Rishonim* and *Ahronim* relevant to important contemporary topics central to our lives, including the current world scene, the battle between Yishmael and Esav, survival through Torah and acts of kindness, *Shemoneh Esrei* as a life preserver, and isolation and redemption. Without doubt, this book fills a need and will enlighten many English-speaking readers, who are sure to benefit from learning about how these issues are dealt with in *Tanach* and the words of *Hazal*.

 The publication of this book is another of R. Neuberger's valuable endeavors for the benefit of the Jewish community. It is my pleasure to bless the Neubergers, Yisrael ben Malkah and Lea bas Rachel, with long, healthy, and happy lives and the ability to continue their work on behalf of the community. May they see great *nahat* from all of their children and grandchildren, who have built homes of Torah and *yirat Shamayim*.

Rabbi Yaakov Hillel

RABBI NAFTALI JAEGER
*Rosh HaYeshiva*

5 Iyar, 5779 (2019)

There is a verse in the prophecies of Amos concerning the Future Time that foretells: "Behold, days will come—thus says the L-rd G-d—when I shall send a famine in the land, not a hunger for bread nor a thirst for water, but only to hear the words of G-d."

The *Midrash Rabbah* teaches that "ten famines have come upon the world, and another will eventually come upon the world in the Future Time"—and proceeds to cite the above-quoted verse. In our days we can patently observe that hunger: our brethren, even though they may have been distant from a life of Torah, experience a lack of spiritual nourishment and seek and yearn to hear the Word of G-d.

Nevertheless, the above-quoted prophetic promise goes on to say: "They will wander from sea to sea, from the north and to the east and seek their way in search of the Word of G-d, *but they will not find it.*"

Now, after such a prolonged search, why will they not find it?

The answer has been given by the men of stature who preceded our generation: Precisely because those seekers have wandered from sea to sea and from the north and to the east, they will not find the Torah—because "it is neither in the heavens nor on the other side of the sea." Rather, "you will seek the L-rd your G-d from there and you will find Him, if you seek Him with all your heart and with all your soul." That is to say: In order to hear and receive the Word of G-d, one must seek Him *from there*—that is, from places in which people study Torah, in the company of scholars and of those who seek its wisdom.

In this spirit, R. Moshe Alshech notes that in the Holy Tongue, the verb meaning "you shall seek" is in the plural, whereas the verb meaning "you will find" is in the singular—as if to narrow down the finders to those who seek in places of Torah scholarship.

And here, my dearly-loved Reb Yisroel Neuberger is a man who is alive to the question and answer of the Sages: "What should a man do in order to be spared from the birth pangs of *Mashiach*? Let him engage in studying Torah and in doing acts of loving-kindness!" Reb Yisroel is widely known

*(continued on next page)*

שאר ישוב
SH'OR YOSHUV
INSTITUTE

ONE CEDARLAWN AVENUE • LAWRENCE, NY 11559 • (516) 239-9002 • FAX: (516) 239-9003

**RABBI NAFTALI JAEGER**
*Rosh HaYeshiva*

*(continued from previous page)*

for his wonderful books in the local language, and for his weekly articles that open the eyes of their readers to G-d's words. Moreover, he and his esteemed wife practice *gemilus chassadim* not only in their home. Rather, like Avraham Avinu and Sarah Imeinu as characterized by Rambam, they assemble groups of people in one place after another and speak with them, bringing them to the path of truth and encouraging them, until they find their place among the wellsprings of Torah and the awe of Heaven. And by virtue of their love and respect for Torah sages, Reb Yisroel and his wife have been blessed with a Torah-true home, and their children's marriage partners are from Torah-true families.

My friend has now brought out another book, whose aim is to rouse readers to the path that we should follow in this era of the approaching birth pangs of *Mashiach*. I am certain that his readers will take its message seriously and will focus their lives towards a genuine Torah life.

Reb Yisroel has made our *beis midrash* the center of his study sessions and of his *davenen,* and radiates a positive influence on those around him. It is with great pleasure, therefore, that I offer my humble blessings to him and to his good lady—that they should be privileged to enjoy ongoing *nachas* from all of their offspring, together with good health, peace of mind, and the joy of the Torah.

In our own lives may we be privileged to personally experience the words with which *Rambam* concludes his *Hilchos Melachim:* "The Sages and prophets did not yearn for the Era of *Mashiach* in order that [the Jewish people] should rule over the entire world, nor in order that they should have dominion over the gentiles, nor that they should be exalted by them, nor in order that they should eat, drink and celebrate. Rather, their aspiration was that [the Jewish people] should be free to engage in the Torah and its wisdom, without anyone to oppress or disturb them, and thus be found worthy of life in the World to Come."

And I can vouch for the fact that this is how our author and his family live their lives.

With respect to the author, and in anticipation of the Redemption,

*Naftali HaLevi Jaeger*

שאר ישוב
SH'OR YOSHUV
INSTITUTE

ONE CEDARLAWN AVENUE • LAWRENCE, NY 11559 • (516) 239-9002 • FAX: (516) 239-9003

בס"ד

שמואל קמנצקי
Rabbi S. Kamenetsky

2018 Upland Way
Philadelphia, PA 19131

Home: 215-473-2798
Study: 215-473-1212

*[Handwritten Hebrew letter]*

My dearly esteemed friend, Reb Yisroel Neuberger

I recently received your valuable book, which highlights the obligation of our generation to recognize that our Righteous *Mashiach* will soon arrive, and that at that time the nations of the world will also recognize that we are "the sons of kings."

Your book points out that since the Redemption is at hand, we are duty-bound to see to it that all of our actions should be appropriate to the noble conduct of the "the sons of kings."

Accordingly, I earnestly hope that your book will succeed in inspiring our people to be prepared in this spirit to greet our Righteous *Mashiach*.

With heartfelt blessings for success,

*Shmuel Kamenetsky*

בס״ד

## Rabbi Zev Leff

*Rabbi of Moshav Matityahu*
*Rosh HaYeshiva—Yeshiva Gedola Matityahu*

## הרב זאב לף

מרא דאתרא מושב מתתיהו
ראש הישיבה—ישיבה גדולה מתתיהו

D.N. Modiin 71917    Tel: 08-976-1138 טל׳    Fax: 08-976-5326 פקס׳    ד.נ. מודיעין 71917

Dear Friends,

    I have read portions of "Survival Handbook for the Days Before Moshiach" by Roy S. Neuberger. The author presents an overview of the world situation putting it into the perspective of our sages as to what the situation will be prior to the coming of Moshiach. He then presents how one can successfully navigate himself to survive "Chevlay Moshiach" the "Birth Pangs" of this era, through Torah and acts of kindness. He concludes with a discussion of **Shmoneh Esrei** as a guide to use in facing the trials and tribulations of this era.

    I found this work based on solid Torah sources, interesting, informative, and inspiring.

    This work can have the effect of solid mussar to wake one up and inspire one to intensify one's connection to Hashem Yisborach through Torah, chesed and tefillah.

    I commend the author for contributing yet another quality presentation added to his previous works and in many places culled from them. I pray that Hashem grants him and his family life and health and the wherewithal to continue to merit the community with further works.

                                               Sincerely,
                                               With Torah blessings

                                               Rabbi Zev Leff

בס"ד

הרב אהרן מרדכי בראפמאן זצ"ל
מנהל (תש"ל-תשע"ז)

**Rabbi Yechiel I. Perr**
*Rosh HaYeshiva*

**Rabbi Mordechai Miller**
*Menahel*

**Rabbi Eli Goldgrab**
*General Studies Principal*

**Rabbi Shayeh Kohn**
*Executive Director*

25 Nissan 5779
April 30, 2019

Dear Reb Yisroel, שליט"א

    Thank you for showing me the draft of your newest *Survival Hand Book for the Days Before Moshiach*.

    I see that in this work you share with your readers a lifetime of experience. A lifetime of growth in knowledge of Torah and in yiras shomayim. A lifetime of living inspired and of inspiring others.

    The greatest z'chus that one can have is doing something to benefit Klal Yisroel.

You have this z'chus.

ביחידות יחיאל פרר

Rabbi Yechiel Perr

**Rabbi I. Scheiner**
*Dean of Kamenitzer Yeshiva*
**51 Zephania St., Jerusalem**
*Tel. (972-2) 532-2512; 532-3664*
*Cell. (972)533-196-968*

הרב יצחק שיינר
ראש ישיבת קמניץ
רחוב צפני' 51, ירושלים
טל. 02-532-2512; 02-532-3664
0533-196-968

בס"ד

אך הצלם

To Reb Yisroel Neuberger שי'

Blessings for the new sefer, called "Survival Handbook". May it be of great use to all who need it.

Sincerely,
יצחק שיינר

Rabbi Eliyahu Schneider
Congregation Zichron Shmuel - Ohel Moshe
3116 Avenue L
Brooklyn, NY 11210
718-258-9454

אליהו חיים שניידער
קהל זכרון שמואל - אהל משה
ברוקלין. נ־י.

ט"ו אייר תשע

It is well known that there are thirteen principles of faith, known as the "Ani Maamin". They all express statements of believing in the foundations of Judaism. However, the twelfth principle is unique. After expressing the belief in the coming of Moshiach, we add, "and even though he may delay, nevertheless, I yearn every day for his arrival." Why is this addition necessary? Doesn't it suffice to mention our belief in Moshiach? The answer is, explains the Brisker Rav ztz"l, that it is not enough to believe in the coming of Moshiach, but to actually anticipate his arrival, with an acute awareness that he may come at any moment, an awareness that demands an anticipation to his arrival.

The truly amazing changes, upheavals, discoveries, and dangers of recent times are opportunities sent by HaShem, to anticipate the arrival of Moshiach. But as the Mesilas Yesharim writes, "everything in this world is a test," and we have the free will to ignore HaShem's messages and to treat this fascinating era as merely "another" segment of history.

This is exactly the importance of this special book. I have read the entire book and I feel that it has the ability to open the eyes of the beginner in Judaism as well as the Talmudic scholar to the fact that HaShem is coordinating the events of our times and begging us to prepare for the Geulah through our increased Torah learning, praying, and love for our fellow Jews. As the Chofetz Chaim writes, the arrival of Moshiach is compared to a wedding, and HaShem gives us one last chance to be properly "dressed" for the wedding.

We owe great gratitude to Mr. Yisroel Neuberger, for deciding to use his G-d gifted talents for Klal Yisroel. May we merit to change from being mere "believers" in Moshiach, to becoming true "anticipators" of Moshiach, as we eagerly await his imminent arrival, BIMHEIRA BIYAMEINU, AMEN!

אליהו חיים שניידער
Eliyahu C. Schneider

**Rabbi Yecheskel Weinfeld**
Beis HaMidrash Lev Avrohom
18 Ramat Hagolan, Jerusalem

יחזקאל שרגא וויינפלד
בית המדרש לב אברהם
ירושלים עיה"ק ת"ו

בס"ד ראש חודש הגאולה, ה'אמב"י.

ידידי אלופי החכם הנכבד, איש חי רב פעלים, רבי ישראל נעדמה שליט"א אשר אני בביתו זה כבר, הריני לציין כחיים הלא פעולות גדולים אשר הוא עוגג להגיג לאוור עולם לזיכוי את הרבים. והנה בדמיו לגדרים דרך צלם ואגלם בחיים את הדברים על ידידי היקר, כי ידועני דו הוא באהר האהבת אמת אל השוה דרא קדמאין על ידידי היקר, כי ידועני דו הוא האגונה והמפגיע ישועות, וראוי הדול אהדה, אהדה הוא אהדת התורה ואהדה ישראל, והוא חזק וקורא דעת ה' אל עולם, רצוי לו לרבנת, גלתך המצוה אחמות לכדת לכן על ישראל לאדיבן שתמצאים, לאמרים שישאיר או חד נפלטין על הדנואה. יתן ה' ויראה רבכת בעמלו, ויפמת לאוהר לדהל למין הבלום ולישר הגשמים והנפשים את הקיים והפנים ורפני לרפאי, ובפי בזה בישר וגשאולכו וקבור לנ?של דגרית גינה. אכי"ר.

הכות בליבה
[חתימה]

*Before Moshiach comes, Hashem will stretch a rope from one end of the world to the other and shake it vigorously. Those who hold on tightly will survive. Those who let go won't. These turbulent times are testing us in our faith in Hashem.*

## We must hold on tightly until the end.

(The Chofetz Chaim)

# TABLE OF CONTENTS

Acknowledgments . . . . . . . . . . . . . . . . . . . . . . . . . . . . . . . . . . XXV
*Chapter 1:* You Shall Be a Blessing . . . . . . . . . . . . . . . . . . . . . . . . . . . 1
*Chapter 2:* A Beginning…Not an End . . . . . . . . . . . . . . . . . . . . . . . 9
*Chapter 3:* The World Scene Today . . . . . . . . . . . . . . . . . . . . . . . .23
*Chapter 4:* The Battle between Yishmael and Eisav . . . . . . . . . . . . . 42
Chapter 5: Survival through Torah . . . . . . . . . . . . . . . . . . . . . . . . .56
*Chapter 6:* Survival through Acts of Kindness . . . . . . . . . . . . . . . . . . .74
*Chapter 7:* Shemoneh Esreh as a Life Preserver . . . . . . . . . . . . . . . . . .93
*Chapter 8:* Isolation and Redemption . . . . . . . . . . . . . . . . . . . . . . .137
Epilogue . . . . . . . . . . . . . . . . . . . . . . . . . . . . . . . . . . . . . . . . . .157
Glossary . . . . . . . . . . . . . . . . . . . . . . . . . . . . . . . . . . . . . . . . . .161

# ACKNOWLEDGMENTS

I am privileged to know many great rabbis who have endorsed this book and our work in general. I want to express my gratitude to the following Torah leaders who have written letters of approbation (in alphabetical order): Rabbi Yaakov Bender, Rabbi Yitzchak Berkovits, Rabbi Shlomo Bussu, Rabbi Dovid Cohen, Rabbi Eytan Feiner, Rabbi Yaakov Feitman, Rabbi Yaakov Moshe Hillel, Rabbi Naftali Jaeger, Rabbi Shmuel Kamenetsky, Rabbi Zev Leff, Rabbi Yechiel Perr, Rabbi Yitzchak Scheiner, Rabbi Eliyahu Schneider, and Rabbi Yechezkel Shraga Weinfeld.

One unique person, Reb Tsemach Glenn, whom my wife and I have known since he was our son's yeshiva classmate, is well known in the Torah world. Since the publication of my first book, *From Central Park to Sinai: How I Found My Jewish Soul*, almost twenty years ago, Reb Tsemach has led me to many Torah luminaries, some of whom I would not have met otherwise, and has otherwise helped me put words into print. May Hashem bless him and his family.

There is an *ish anav*, a humble person and *talmid chacham*, who has helped me greatly with this book, trying to ensure its accuracy, helping me refine Torah concepts, finding sources and providing numerous citations that have added depth and strength to the book. That person is Rabbi Eliyahu Schneider, *shlita*. May Hashem bless him and his family.

I want to thank and recognize the *talmidei chachamim* who have had the patience to learn with me and try to pump Torah wisdom into what sometimes seems to me a hopelessly muddy brain! I have had and continue to have the privilege of learning Torah with (in alphabetical order) Rabbi Shaul Geller, Rabbi Moshe Grossman, and Rabbi Yehuda

Schiff. I also want to pay tribute to those who taught me and our family long ago, from the beginning of our Jewish journey: Rebbetzin Esther Jungreis, *a"h*, Rabbi Meshulam Jungreis, *zt"l*, Rabbi Yaakov Jungreis, *shlita*, and Rabbi Shlomo Gertzulin, *shlita*.

I am blessed to have a *choshuve* publishing team with whom it is a pleasure to work. I refer, of course, to Mosaica Press and its directors, Rabbi Yaacov Haber, *shlita*, and Rabbi Doron Kornbluth, *shlita*, as well as Rabbi Reuven Butler, *shlita*. Rayzel Broyde's cover design and graphics are beautiful and brilliant. I am so impressed with the careful professionalism of the editing under the direction of Mrs. Sherie Gross. Their dedication and insight have greatly enhanced this book. May Hashem bless them and enable them to continue disseminating His Torah with great success!

My *eishes chayil* and I met at a young age. We both knew there had to be a true path, and together we searched for it. Since the publication of *From Central Park to Sinai: How I Found My Jewish Soul*, we have spoken together publicly to audiences in many countries. She is the first editor of everything I write. May we, together with our children and their families, see the day when Hashem shines "a new light on Tziyon."[1]

Thank you, Hashem, for the blessings You constantly shower upon us! May all Your children give You increasing *nachas* until the time—may it come soon!—when the Shechinah returns from exile, Moshiach ben Dovid leads our people home, and the Beis Hamikdash stands forever in glory upon its mountain in the Holy City of Yerushalayim!

Yisroel (Roy) Neuberger<br>
Iyar 5779

---

1   "*Ohr chadash al tziyon ta'ir*" in *tefillas Shacharis*.

*Chapter 1*

# YOU SHALL BE A BLESSING

*Rabbi Elazar was asked by his students, "What can a person do to be spared the travails of Moshiach?" [And he responded], "One should occupy himself in [the study of] Torah and in acts of kindness."*[1]

My heart is filled with trepidation at the immediate future of Klal Yisrael and indeed the entire world. The world depends on the blessings that the Jewish People bring into it. As Hashem said to Avraham Avinu, "You shall be a blessing…and all the families of the earth shall bless themselves by you."[2]

The chaotic, violent, polluted world we live in will one day—I believe soon—become like Gan Eden again. Hashem created a perfect world. We destroyed it. But Hashem will rescue us. "When the wicked bloom like grass and all the doers of iniquity blossom, it is to destroy them until eternity."[3]

Rescue and renewal are not only possible, but they are a certainty. As we say every day, "Blessed are You, Hashem, our Lord, King of the Universe…Who illuminates the earth and those who dwell upon it,

---

1  *Sanhedrin* 98b.
2  *Bereishis* 12:2–3.
3  *Tehillim* 92.

with compassion, and, in His goodness, renews daily, perpetually, the work of Creation."[4]

Today, we feel separated from our Creator. But He is merciful and He will undoubtedly rescue those who desire to be rescued, just as He rescued our ancestors in Egypt. We have to try to come close to Him.

"Hashem…bestows beneficial kindnesses and…recalls the kindnesses of the Avos and [will] bring a redeemer to their children's children for His Name's sake, with love."[5] The language of this *berachah*, written by our rabbis thousands of years ago with Divine inspiration and incorporated into our daily prayers, is deeply revealing. Notice how it ends: Hashem will "bring a redeemer" even if we don't merit him! How do we know this? Because it says "for His Name's sake, with love," which hints at deliverance even if we do not merit it completely. This is an enormous kindness to us, a kindness beyond understanding.

The source for this is the passage in *Yechezkel*, which says:

> I [will take] pity on My Holy Name, which the House of Israel had desecrated among nations…. Therefore, say to the House of Israel…. It is not for your sake that I act, Oh House of Israel, but for My Holy Name that you have desecrated among the nations…. I will sanctify My great Name that is desecrated among the nations…and I will become sanctified through you before their eyes. I will take you from [among] the nations and gather you from all the lands and I will bring you to your own soil. Then I will sprinkle pure water upon you, that you may become cleansed…. I will give you a new heart and put a new spirit within you…You will dwell in the land that I gave to your forefathers; you will be a people to Me and I will be a G-d to you….[6]

The Chofetz Chaim states concerning the apparent delay in the end of our exile,

---

4   *Shacharis.*
5   *Shemoneh Esreh.*
6   *Yechezkel* 36:21ff.

> *Hashem's redemption can occur in the blink of an eye.... However, the reason [for the delay] is clear to me that Hashem is somewhat delaying the...redemption in order to give us time to prepare ourselves for the coming of our righteous Moshiach, that we should not go out to greet him while naked of Torah and mitzvos....*[7]

This is a book about the coming of Moshiach ben Dovid, the Jewish king who is going to rescue not only Klal Yisrael but the entire world. When we are rescued, everyone will be rescued, because we are the blessing of the world. Moshiach is going to introduce a world of peace and justice that will never end. Our prophets have made this clear and, with Hashem's help, we will discuss these prophecies in more detail later. Deep down, many of us realize this. Indeed, many non-Jews understand—in some way, deep down—that the Jews are central to the world's rectification. When we are not doing our job as a spiritual nation, the world becomes angry at us. This is one reason there is anti-Semitism.

The *Beis Halevi* discusses this phenomenon. He quotes Dovid HaMelech, who praises Hashem, because "He turned [our enemies'] heart to hate His people...."[8] Why would Dovid HaMelech praise Hashem for causing our enemies to hate us?

The Egyptians' hatred toward us was caused by our ancestors' abandonment of circumcision so that we would not appear different from the Egyptians. This attempt to assimilate into Egyptian culture caused Hashem to arouse hatred against us in order to "keep the peoples apart and facilitate [our ancestors'] redemption! We now understand," continues the *Beis Halevi*, "why [Dovid HaMelech] depicts the turning of the Egyptians against B'nei Yisrael as a manifestation of Hashem's kindness toward His people."

And the *Beis Halevi* continues, "We see in our own times how anti-Semitism is constantly intensifying.... The more Jews try to bridge the

---

7 Chofetz Chaim, letter 18.
8 *Tehillim* 105.

natural gap between themselves and others by abandoning the distinctive mitzvos of the Torah, the more Hashem must place an unnatural gap between them."[9]

In other words, if we are not remaining faithful to the Torah, Hashem sends non-Jews to motivate us to come closer to Him! This is the classic reason for anti-Semitism!

The late Rabbi Yerucham Levovitz, mashgiach of the Mirrer Yeshiva, was in Poland before World War II, and he saw the German preparations for future concentration camps. He said the following powerful words: "The Jews stopped believing in Gehinnom, so Hashem decided to bring Gehinnom into this world. Not the whole Gehinnom, but a little bit of it…. [The Third Reich was] a foretaste; a little bit of Gehinnom."[10]

The Gemara quotes the opening *pasuk* in *Eichah*: "She sits in solitude."[11] What is the reason for Israel's eternal isolation?

> *Rava said in the name of Rabbi Yochanan: Hashem said, "Israel shall dwell securely, alone, in a land of grain and wine, just like Yaakov. Even its heavens shall drip with dew."*[12]

The original intention of Hashem was that we should dwell with honor, alone in our own land, but now that we have sinned and are in exile, "their dwelling shall be alone."[13]

Hashem meant that B'nei Yisrael should dwell "alone in the Land of Israel, apart from the negative influences of the gentiles and their culture. But, instead, the Jews strove to emulate the gentiles…and merge with them. Hashem therefore…caused the gentiles to despise and reject the Jews."[14]

Although this is very hard, it is all for our welfare.

Hashem is separating His children from the other nations.

---

9   *Beis Halevi* on the Torah, *Parashas Shemos*, pages 10ff.
10  Rabbi Avigdor Miller, Purim *derashah*, 1981.
11  *Sanhedrin* 104a.
12  *Devarim* 33:28.
13  Ibid.
14  Artscroll commentary based on the *Netziv*, *Meishiv Davar* 1:44; *Haamek Davar* to *Devarim* 33:28.

A time is coming in which the world will be pure, sunlit, and happy.

> *A staff will grow from the stump of Yishai, and a shoot will grow from his roots. The spirit of Hashem will rest upon him, a spirit of wisdom and understanding, a spirit of counsel and strength, a spirit of knowledge and fear of Hashem.... The wolf will lie down with the lamb and the leopard will lie down with the kid...and a young child will lead them.... They will neither injure nor destroy in all of My sacred mountain, for the earth will be as filled with knowledge of Hashem as water covers the sea bed....It shall be on that day that the L-rd will once again show His hand to acquire the remnant of His people, who will have remained.... He will raise a banner for the nations and assemble the castaways of Israel, and He will gather in the dispersed ones of Yehudah from the four corners of the earth....*[15]

At that time, people will respect each other and the word of Hashem will rule. That word will radiate to the whole world from Yerushalayim. The Jewish People will be honored and exalted, recognized as the Children of Hashem and the source of all blessing. All tears will be wiped away. Sickness and death, which began when Adam and Chavah were expelled from Gan Eden, will be banished. Indeed, we will return to Gan Eden.

The *Rambam* says:

> *Since the time of Creation, man has had the ability to choose freely whether to be righteous or wicked. This will be so throughout all of the Torah era, so that they may gain merit by choosing good and deserve punishment if they want evil. But in the days of Moshiach, it will be natural for them to choose the good. Their heart will not want anything inappropriate; they will have no desire for it at all.... At that time, man will revert to his state before the sin of Adam, who did by nature*

---

15   *Yeshayah* 11.

> *what was proper to do…. This is what is meant by, "Behold, days are coming, says Hashem, when I will forge with the House of Israel and the House of Yehudah a new covenant, unlike the covenant I forged with their forefathers…. For this is the covenant that I will forge with the House of Israel after those days, says Hashem. I will have put the Torah inside them and written it upon their hearts…."[16]*

Considering the reality of our day-to-day lives, it isn't easy to believe in such changes. Do you believe this can happen?

Did the Jews in Egypt believe they would escape and stand with Hashem at Har Sinai?

The entire history of the Jewish People to this day is logically impossible, but it is reality. The existence of the Jewish nation as a cohesive, identifiable entity after two thousand years of worldwide dispersion among cruel enemies seems impossible. If we think the complete redemption cannot or will not happen, we are wrong. It is coming—but we must cling to Hashem and His Torah very tightly, like a life preserver!

All our sources make clear that we are going to return to Gan Eden. But the world is very likely going to go through rough times and momentous changes before we get there. The idea is to hang on to Hashem and His Torah. He will hold our hand, and we will get there.

The Chofetz Chaim explained the term *"chevlei Moshiach,"* which means "birth pangs of Moshiach." He linked the term *"chevlei"* to the word *"chevel,"* meaning "rope." Here is what he said:

> *Before Moshiach comes, Hashem will stretch a rope from one end of the world to the other and shake it violently. Those who hold on tightly will survive. Those who let go won't survive. These turbulent times are testing our trust in Hashem. We must hold on tightly until the end.[17]*

---

16   Ramban on *Devarim* 30:6, quoting *Yirmiyah* 31:30–32.
17   From an article by Rabbi Yitzchok Tzvi Schwartz, *Yated Ne'eman*, March 13, 2015.

Dovid HaMelech said:

> *Whoever sits in the refuge of the Most High, he shall dwell in the shadow of the Almighty. I will say of Hashem, "He is my refuge and my fortress, my G-d. I will trust in Him" that He will deliver you from the ensnaring trap and from devastating pestilence. With His pinions He will cover you, and beneath His wings you will be protected. His truth is shield and armor. You shall not be afraid of the terror of night, nor of the arrow that flies by day, nor the pestilence that walks in gloom, nor the destroyer who lays waste at noon. Let a thousand encamp at your side and a myriad at your right hand, but to you they shall not approach. You will merely peer with your eyes and you will see the retribution of the wicked. Because [you said], "You, Hashem, are my refuge," you have made the Most High your dwelling place. No evil will befall you, nor will any plague come near your tent...*[18]

Anyone who clings to the culture of the surrounding nations is clinging to something that is going to disappear, just like the culture of ancient Egypt disappeared along with those who clung to it.

> *So says Hashem: Cursed is the man who trusts in people and makes mortals his strength and turns his heart away from Hashem. He will be like a lone tree in the wilderness and will not see when goodness comes; he will dwell in the arid desert, in a sulfurous uninhabited land. Blessed is the man who trusts in Hashem. Then Hashem will be his security. He will be like a tree that is planted near water, which will spread its roots alongside brooks and will not see when heat comes, whose foliage will be ever fresh, who will not worry in years of drought and will never stop producing fruit.*[19]

---

18  *Tehillim* 91.
19  *Yirmiyah* 17:5–8.

On fast days, we read the following towering words in *tefillas Minchah*:

> *So says Hashem to the barren ones who observe My Shabbos and choose what I desire and grasp My covenant tightly. In My House and within My walls I shall give them a place and renown better than sons and daughters; eternal renown shall I give them, never to be cut down, and the aliens who join Hashem to serve Him and to love the Name of Hashem to become His servants, whoever guards the Shabbos against desecration and grasps My covenant tightly, I shall bring them to My holy mountain and I shall gladden them in My house of prayer, their elevation offerings and their feast offerings will find favor on My altar, for My House shall be a house of prayer for all the peoples.... The words of my Lord, Hashem...Who gathers in the dispersed of Israel, "I shall gather to him even more than those already gathered."*[20]

We have to be prepared. We have to survive. We have to know what is ahead. If we do our utmost to prepare for the world of Torah that is just over the horizon, then with Hashem's help, we will live to see it.

---

20  *Yeshayah* 56:4–8.

*Chapter 2*

# A BEGINNING...NOT AN END

We are now approaching the end of history as we know it, but if we would have accurate vision, we would see it more as a beginning than an end. Shabbos is the end of the week, but it is more like a beginning—a door leading to a greater world.

> *To welcome the Shabbos, come, let us go.*
> *For it is the source of blessing.*
> *From the beginning, from antiquity she was honored.*
> *Last in deed, but first in thought.*
> *Shake off the dust, arise!*
> *Don your splendid clothes, My people.*
> *Through [Moshiach], the son of Yishai,*
> *from Beis Lechem.*
> *Draw near to my soul...redeem it!*[1]

Yetzias Mitzrayim was the end of our first *galus*, but it was more a beginning than an end. This was the beginning of our birth as the nation belonging to Hashem and living by His Torah.

---

1  *Lechah Dodi.*

In the same way, the end of the era in which we are living now can be characterized as more a beginning than an end, and, if we view it in that light, that may be the way in which we are able to survive the transition and enter the new world that is just over the horizon.

This is why the current period is characterized as "*chevlei Moshiach*," the birth pangs of Moshiach.

This birth will be equal to the greatest moments in the history of Creation, equal to the day at Har Sinai when Hashem gave us the Torah. This is the Shabbos of history, the seventh millennium. This is a huge moment.

It is so huge that it requires a realization on our part that we are going to have to let go of the way we have been living and accept what Hashem is bringing to pass, just as we accept Shabbos and let go of the weekdays that precede it.

I do not think that we are prepared.

Many are afraid to contemplate the magnitude of the coming change, which is understandable if we are trying to hang on to the past. This is why it is so important to compare the current moment to the onset of Shabbos or to *yetzias Mitzrayim*, both of which are our gateways to Torah and to eternal closeness with the Ribbono shel Olam.

This is our liberation! This is our redemption!

On this basis, we can find a realistic basis of hope as to how we can survive until the glorious days of Moshiach arrive.

Malachi was the last of the prophets; he wrote just before the close of the age of prophecy. Towards the end of his writings, he stated these words: "Then those who fear Hashem spoke to one another, and Hashem listened and heard, and a book of remembrance was written before Him for those who fear Hashem and who give thought to His Name...."[2]

Noach worked for 120 years constructing the *teivah*. Building this great boat in public was equivalent to announcing that the world was

---

2   *Malachi* 3:16.

about to be destroyed, but no one paid attention. In fact, they ignored or made fun of him.

But he was right.

Nearly all human life was wiped out. The rest of humanity had caused its own destruction by rejecting the rules Hashem had given them to live in this world.

The situation is repeating itself now.

This is occurring in such an obvious way that it is screaming at us from the mountaintops. Even the causes of the *Mabul*—moral degeneration and robbery—are repeating themselves.³

Moral corruption, including "alternative lifestyles," has not only become legalized but has become widely accepted in many countries that consider themselves civilized. The Torah makes it clear that this spells certain doom. Hashem made human beings as man and woman. Hashem said, "It is not good that man be alone. I will make him a helper corresponding to him."⁴ As man's companion, He made woman. This is how Hashem set up the world. Man is not complete without woman, and vice versa. They are *"basar echad*—one flesh."⁵

Through their union, life continues on earth.

If mankind tries to uproot the order in which Hashem made the world, the result is not life but death. Thus, the death of the world through the *Mabul* occurred as a result of moral degradation, as it says: "All flesh had perverted its way on the earth."⁶

"It is taught in a *Beraisa*: The waters of the *Mabul* were harsh…. Rav Chisda said, they acted corruptly and [therefore] with boiling water they were punished."⁷

The accepted way of life of the present generation includes a complete rejection of the order by which Hashem created the world. This phenomenon is occurring in countries around the globe. The behavior

---

3   We know these were the causes of the *Mabul* from the Torah itself and from the classic commentary of our rabbis.
4   *Bereishis* 2:18.
5   Ibid. 2:24.
6   Ibid. 6:12.
7   *Sanhedrin* 108b.

that directly caused the destruction of the world in the time of Noach is recurring, and we are not willing to acknowledge what is happening.

The Written and Oral Torah state clearly that the consequence of this kind of behavior is the destruction of life on this earth. Past a certain point, Hashem will surely not tolerate the corruption of the world He created.

"In the generation that [Moshiach] the son of Dovid will come…the entire [world] will convert to heresy…. for Rabbi Yitzchak said: [Moshiach] will not come until the entire [world] converts to heresy."[8] The Gemara supports that statement with a *pasuk* from the Torah: "All of it has turned white; it is pure."[9] This *pasuk* alludes to the sickness the Torah calls *tzaraas*. According to halachah, when *tzaraas* covers part of a person's body, he is impure, but when it covers his entire body, he is pure.[10] The Gemara is saying that, similarly, "when heresy spreads across the entire world, the time for redemption has come."[11]

If we are not already there, we are getting very close!

The other cause of the *Mabul* was robbery.

> *Now the earth had become corrupt before Hashem, and the earth had become filled with robbery. And Hashem saw the earth and behold it was corrupted…for all flesh had corrupted its way upon the earth. Hashem said to Noach, "The end of all flesh has come before Me…and behold, I am about to destroy them from the earth."*[12]

> *Rabbi Yochanan said: Come and see how great is the power of robbery, for the dor haMabul transgressed everything, yet the decree of their punishment was not sealed upon them until they stretched forth their hands in robbery.*[13]

---

8   Ibid. 97a.
9   *Vayikra* 13:13.
10  *Nega'im* 8:1.
11  *Sanhedrin* 97a.
12  *Bereishis* 6:11.
13  *Sanhedrin* 108a.

Robbery erases the boundaries between people, causing universal hatred and fear. This overturns the ideal of a peaceful relationship among mankind, such as that which is described in the *pasuk*: "They will sit, each man under his vine and under his fig tree, and none will make them afraid...."[14]

Although robbery itself is widespread, as I said above, I would like to suggest another interpretation of the term "robbery" that I believe can be applied to the current world scene, and that is the attempt of the nations of the world to steal the Land of Israel from its rightful owners, who have been given this gift by Hashem, as explained clearly in many passages in the Torah. As Hashem tells Avraham, "I will give to you and your offspring after you the land of your sojourns, the whole of the land of Canaan as an everlasting possession...."[15] Almost the entire world is united in trying to rob us of our G-d-given possession.

This has taken on a different form from the way it was in the past.

> *In the end of days, after Klal Yisrael has returned to their land, the children of Yishmael and the children of Eisav will unite to attack Yerushalayim. They will form a world coalition against the tiny nation of Israel....*"[16]

This is happening in our day. The coalition of world nations, whether descended from Yishmael or from Eisav, are working together to steal the land from the Jews.

Christians and Arabs have been attacking Yerushalayim for millennia, but now, as the final redemption draws near, they are coordinating their attack and acting in concert. The commentary by the *Malbim* cited above, which describes a worldwide coalition that will attempt to appropriate the Land of Israel from Klal Yisrael, predicts that this will happen.

In an article in the newspaper *Hamodia*, military correspondent A. Pe'er reported that "outside elements (including Turkey, Jordan, and

---

14　*Michah* 4:4.
15　*Bereishis* 17:8.
16　*Malbim* on *Yechezkel* 32:17.

Arab organizations, as well as the United Nations and the European Union) are acting to undermine Israel's sovereignty over Eastern Yerushalayim and lay claim to [the Temple Mount]," as well as the grave of Shmuel HaNavi, which is just outside Yerushalayim on the northern border.[17]

Thus, between immorality and robbery, mankind has set the stage for the destruction of the entire world, just as in the days of the *Mabul*. We cannot imagine the suffering involved, but it seems clear that the world is quickly moving in this direction.

It also seems clear, however, that we can try to save ourselves, just as Noach and his family did on the basis of their allegiance to Hashem. But unless we see it coming and understand why it is coming, how will we save ourselves?

I heard a fascinating insight from Rabbi Shlomo Bussu: Dasan and Aviram rebelled against Moshe and Aharon in Egypt and in the *midbar* and were punished when the earth opened up and swallowed them. If they were such evil people, why were they able to survive *Makkas Choshech* when so many of B'nei Yisrael perished?

As Rabbi Bussu explained, the fact that Dasan and Aviram were aware of the coming redemption was enough merit on their part to allow them to leave Egypt.

We have to be aware of what is happening in order to survive!

But often it seems we don't want to know what is happening.

The prophet says, "You will tell them all these things, but they will not listen to you. You will call to them but they will not answer you."[18]

The Chofetz Chaim chillingly predicted the world scene today:

> *Let's see for ourselves where we are holding today. The Jewish nation is drowning in oceans of sorrow throughout all the lands where we are dispersed. The sanctity of our holy Torah is declining day by day in a way that is shocking,*

---

17  *Hamodia*, February 6, 2019. The grave of Shmuel HaNavi is an extremely strategic point; from there almost all of Yerushalayim is visible.

18  *Yirmiyah* 7:27.

*because of our many sins. On every side, they arise against us to annihilate us. And they impose on us awesome decrees and regulations that touch upon our very existence and the existence of the Torah. The new rising generation is being educated without any Torah or faith, and they have become children who contemptuously repudiate Hashem and His Torah. The pillars and basic foundation of our Torah have been trashed as valueless, G-d forbid, to a large segment of our Jewish brothers.*

*If this situation, G-d forbid, should continue for a few more years, who knows where the state of Judaism will be, G-d forbid. Human logic dictates that the time of the coming of our righteous Moshiach cannot be far off, because we find ourselves at a level that cannot possibly be worse and lowlier than this. It is within our ability to expedite the redemption by returning to Hashem in sincere teshuvah and preparing ourselves in Torah and chessed.*

*That being so, my brothers and friends who are zealous to uphold the word of Hashem and His Torah, who worry over the existence of our nation and our holy Torah, all who are affected by the fear of Heaven and believe with complete faith in the coming of Moshiach, we must prepare ourselves with all of our might for the coming of our righteous Moshiach, each person to the best of his ability, some in Tanach, some in Mishnah, and some in Gemara, in order to merit the true, complete redemption and enable ourselves to greet Moshiach in happiness.*

*Anyone who does not take to heart these words of ours, should understand clearly that he is putting his life at risk, and in the future he will have to give an accounting and reckoning at his trial, G-d forbid, because at that time it will be clearly evident and will be publicized for everyone to see, who were the people who prepared themselves for his arrival and how did they prepare themselves in Torah and chessed, and who*

> *did not prepare himself for his arrival. What emerges from all of the words mentioned above is that all of us, from the smallest to the greatest, must strengthen ourselves in those things that are critical to the onset of the geulah: Torah and good deeds.[19]*

This striking statement, written about ninety years ago, describes our current situation clearly and starkly. We have to understand what we are facing. We have the power of life in our hands.

I want to present a parable which illustrates our situation:

> *Suppose there are twin brothers lying together in the womb. They ask each other what will happen to them once they leave the womb. They would not be able to form any conception whatsoever of what awaits them—all the things their eyes would see and their ears would hear on earth. Let us imagine that one of them believes in the tradition that he had received—that there was a future life beyond the womb—while the other, a "rational" being, would only accept what his own intelligence could grasp, and he, accordingly, would only acknowledge the existence of what he experienced of "this world" alone. The two would disagree and argue, very much as men do on earth, some believing that man continues to live, others denying that man has any life other than in the world of the present.*
>
> *Suppose that the "believing" brother were to repeat what had been transmitted to him—that, with their emergence from the womb, they would enter a new and more spacious realm, that they would eat through their mouths, see distant objects with their eyes and hear with their ears, that their legs would straighten, that they would stand erect and traverse vast distances on a gigantic nurturing earth, replete with oceans*

---

19  *Maamar Chizuk Ha'Emunah*, printed in Kislev 5690/1929 in *Likutei Maamarim U'Michtavim* of the Chofetz Chaim.

and rivers, while above them would stretch a starry sky. The other, who only believed in what he could sense, would jeer at this brother's naivete in indulging in such fantasies. He would retort that only a fool would believe all of this nonsense, which makes no sense to the rational mind. The more the "believer" would elaborate on what they would encounter in the next world, the more the "rational" brother would mock and ridicule him.

The believing brother would ask, "What then, my enlightened brother, do you believe is in store for us when we leave the womb?"

The rational brother would reply, "Simple and obvious. Once this enclosure opens and you are torn away from this world where your food and drink are provided, you will fall into an abyss from which there is no return. You might as well never have existed at all."

In the heat of their argument, the womb suddenly opens. The "naïve" brother slips and falls outside. Remaining within, the other brother is shattered by the "tragedy" that has overtaken his brother!

"Brother, where are you? How did you manage to fall to your destruction?! Your folly in believing that these contractions were birth pangs caused your downfall. That is why you did not clutch at anything to stop yourself."

As he moans over his misfortune, his ears catch the cries of his brother, and he trembles. To him, this spells the end, the last gasp of his dying brother.

Outside, at that very moment, joy and celebration fill the room.

"Mazal Tov! Mazal Tov! We have a son!"[20]

---

20  Adapted from *Gesher HaChaim*: *The Bridge of Life*, by Rabbi Y.M. Tuchazinski.

The process by which the final redemption will arrive is referred to as "*chevlei Moshiach,*" the birth pangs of Moshiach. Right now, we are unable to imagine the world of Moshiach unless we avail ourselves of the tradition of our rabbis as embodied in the Written and Oral Torah. It will be a world beyond our imagining. But right now, we are in pain, and this is the pain which has been predicted as the prelude to the coming of Moshiach.

Just as a woman gives birth in pain, so too the advent of Moshiach will be painful. In fact, the pain of childbirth was decreed when Adam and Chavah rebelled against Hashem in Gan Eden, when Hashem said to Chavah, "I will greatly increase your suffering and your childbearing. In pain shall you bear children."[21] In Gan Eden, before Adam and Chavah rebelled against Hashem, a woman would conceive and give birth "immediately and painlessly. Now that would change. Conception would not be automatic, and there would be an extended period of pregnancy and labor pains."[22]

The scenario for the advent of Moshiach was already in place at the dawn of history.

I would like to suggest that, like the scenario described in this parable, the world that will follow the advent of Moshiach will be totally unlike the world we are experiencing now. Our fear of that world, our refusal to believe in its very existence, may actually inhibit its coming.

The coming days, months, and years will certainly bring Moshiach.

But what will happen between now and then?

The world will certainly return to perfection, as it was when Hashem created it and before mankind ruined it. Moshiach is hidden and we do not know when he is coming, but, as we just noted, the Chofetz Chaim writes: "Human logic dictates that the time of the coming of our righteous Moshiach cannot be far off."

---

21  *Bereishis* 3:16.
22  *Seforno.*

All mouths will undoubtedly drop when his identity is revealed, just the way his brothers' mouths dropped open when Yosef said the amazing words, *"Ani Yosef*—I am Yosef."[23]

It was the same way when Hashem told Shmuel HaNavi to anoint Dovid as king of Israel. All mouths dropped open, because no one, including Dovid's own father and brothers, suspected for a moment that he was destined to become king. Far from it; he was suspected as a thief, an illegitimate child, or even a non-Jew. He was suspected of every bad thing, but he was, in fact, the purest of the pure.

"Sent away from his home, a pariah in the community at large, Dovid found rich pasture and clear, flowing water for his soul, which thirsted for Hashem, in the wilderness to which he fled. There, where no one knew him or saw him, he sought to draw close to Hashem."[24] Dovid spoke to Hashem in purity, just like Avraham, Moshe, and others who separated themselves from corruption.

When Moshiach comes and the Beis Hamikdash is rebuilt, Hashem will usher in an era of redemption, and the world will be pure as it was before mankind destroyed it. "The People of Israel, created to correct Adam's sin, will ultimately make Gan Eden greater than the one from which Adam [and Chavah were] expelled. In the future, Gan Eden will have such perfection that even the possibility of sin will be eliminated."[25]

But until that moment, it seems clear that we may have to endure the greatest upheaval in history.

We must prepare.

What stands in the way of that preparation is that we don't want to know about it.

We say *"Shema Yisrael*—Hear O Israel," every day, but are we listening?

We pray that Hashem should save us, but do we believe we need to be saved?

---

23 *Bereishis* 45:3.
24 *Book of Our Heritage*, p. 852.
25 Rabbi Shmuel Elchonen Brog, overview to *The Shabbos Home* by Rabbi Simcha Bunim Cohen.

We are addicted to the surrounding culture and its decadent lifestyle. We cannot contemplate that the surrounding culture will disappear, so we try to think how it can be saved.

Let us consider the words of Rabbi Shimshon Pincus:

> We start to realize what kind of a place the world has become. We live in a "modern" world, but with all its technological advances, including audio recording devices and cameras...the results are shockingly poor. Everything is put to use for the bad. The world was a more beautiful place without modern cameras and their streams of indecent images that now flood the world. And so it is with technology's other products.[26]

Our rabbis warned us about this, but we are not paying attention.

We want to continue to go about our daily routine, but the world as we know it is about to destroy itself. Here is the well-known Mishnah which describes the world decline that will occur at the end of history.

> During Vespasian's campaign [against Yerushalayim] the Sages decreed [a ban] on grooms' wreaths and on the iyrus [a musical instrument]. During Titus' campaign, they decreed a ban on brides' wreaths and that no man may teach his son Greek. During the final campaign, they decreed that a bride may not go forth in a canopy within the city....
>
> When Rabbi Meir died, there ceased to be composers of parables.
>
> When Ben Azai died, there ceased to be diligent [scholars].
>
> Once Ben Zoma died, there ceased to be experts in exegesis.
>
> Once Rabbi Akiva died, the glory of Torah ceased.
>
> Once Rabbi Chanina ben Dosa died, there ceased to be people of deeds.

---

26  *Nefesh Shimshon, Thirteen Principles of Faith*, p. 273.

*Once Rabbi Yose Katonta died, there ceased to be pious men. And why was he called "Katonta"? Because he was the least [katan] of the pious men.*

*Once Rabbi Yochanan ben Zakkai died, the splendor of wisdom ceased.*

*Once Rabban ben Gamliel the Elder died, the glory of Torah ceased (in a different sense from Rabbi Akiva), and purity died, as well as abstinence.*

*Once Rabbi Yishmael ben Pavi died, the splendor of the kehunah ceased.*

*Once Rabbi died, humility ceased, as well as dread of sin.*

*Our rabbis taught: Rabbi Pinchas ben Yair says: From [the time] the Temple was destroyed, chaverim and high-born men have been ashamed, and their heads have been covered, and men of merit have been impoverished. But strong-armed men and slanderers have triumphed, and there is none who seeks and none who searches and none who inquires. Upon whom [then] can we lean? Upon our Father in Heaven!*

*Rabbi Eliezer the Great says: From the day the Beis Hamikdash was destroyed, scholars began to be like schoolteachers and schoolteachers like synagogue attendants and synagogue attendants like [unlearned] commoners and commoners became steadily more impoverished [in wisdom and observance], and there is none who inquires and none who searches. Upon whom can we lean? Upon our Father in Heaven!*

*In the period which will precede the coming of Moshiach, insolence will increase and costs will soar. The vine will yield its fruit, yet wine will be dear, and the government will turn to heresy and there shall be no rebuke. The [erstwhile] meeting place [of Sages] will be used for harlotry and the Galilee will be destroyed and the Gavlan devastated and the people [who dwell] on the borders will wander about from town to town, but they will not be succored. And the wisdom of scribes will decay and those who dread sin will be despised and truth will be absent. Youths will blanch the face of elders; elders will stand in the presence of minors. The son derides his father; a daughter rises against her mother and a daughter-in-law against her mother-in-law; a man's enemies are the people of his household. The face of the generation is like the face of a dog; a son is not abashed [in the presence] of his father.*

*Upon what, then, can we lean? Upon our Father in Heaven!*[27]

---

27   Sotah 49a/b.

*Chapter 3*

# THE WORLD SCENE TODAY

The world scene today is extremely dangerous. It is vital for us to understand this so that we can be prepared for what is coming and save ourselves to the greatest possible extent.

> *For behold: I command! I shall shake the House of Israel among all the nations as one shakes [grain] in a sieve, and no pebble shall fall to the ground. By the sword will all the sinners of My people die, those who say, "The evil will not approach and overtake us!"*[1]

On the other hand, we must remember that the world after the upheaval is going to be beautiful beyond our comprehension. Every Friday night, we sing about the coming of the Holy Shabbos.

> *O Sanctuary of the King, Royal City….*
> *Arise and depart from amidst the upheaval.*
> *Too long have you dwelt in the valley of weeping.*
> *He will shower compassion on you.*
> *Wake up! Wake up! For your light has come. Rise up and shine.*
> *Awaken! Awaken! Utter a song!*

---

1  *Amos* 9:9–10 (haftarah for *Acharei Mos*).

> *The glory of Hashem is revealed on you.*
> *Rightward and leftward you shall spread out mightily.*
> *And you shall extol the might of Hashem.*
> *Through the man descended from Peretz.*
> *Then we shall be glad and mirthful!*[2]

There will come a Shabbos that never ends, as we say, "May the Compassionate One cause us to inherit the day which will be completely a Shabbos!"[3]

We must try to survive, so that we will merit to live in this world that will exist in glory after the redemption, the world described by the words, "*Ki miTziyon teitzei Torah u'dvar Hashem miYerushalayim*—From Tziyon will come forth Torah and the word of Hashem from Yerushalayim."[4]

A day will come when the world is not run from New York or Moscow or Beijing or Wall Street or Silicon Valley or Hollywood or the mysterious place called the internet. At that time, the world will acknowledge Hashem's law, which will emanate from Yerushalayim, but which in fact comes from the Almighty.

"Hashem is King forever and ever, when the nations have perished from the earth."[5] Rabbi Samson Raphael Hirsch explains this in the following way: "One day, when Hashem's sovereignty will be acknowledged everywhere and the earth shall have become 'His earth,' the opposition of the nations…shall disappear from Hashem's world."[6]

That is in the future. Right now, the danger is extreme. The Torah shows us what can happen. Imagine living in Egypt in the days of Moshe. We know that at least four-fifths of B'nei Yisrael perished in *Makkas Choshech*. Some commentators say it was more like one in five hundred who survived.

Can we understand this? Whatever the numbers, this was a holocaust!

---

2   *Lechah Dodi.*
3   *Birkas Hamazon.*
4   *Yeshayah* 2:3.
5   *Tehillim* 10:16.
6   Rabbi Samson Raphael Hirsch on *Tehillim* 10:16.

Why did this happen? *Rashi* says that "there were among that generation wicked individuals who did not wish to depart from Egypt and they died [in *Makkas Choshech*]."[7] But if they had known that Egypt was doomed and that Moshe Rabbeinu would lead them to spiritual and physical glory that would last forever...is it not possible (or even probable) that they would have allied themselves with him and saved their lives?

It is certainly possible.

So too today, when our entire world is threatened, we have a responsibility to ourselves and our families, and really to the entire world, to understand what is happening, so that we can save ourselves and communicate to others what is about to happen.

The story of B'nei Yisrael in ancient Egypt demonstrates that we can save ourselves through spiritual preparation. The Jews who were saved in Biblical Egypt were not saved by swords or other physical weapons, but rather by a spiritual decision to adhere to Hashem and His prophet, Moshe. "Not through [armies] and not through strength, but through My spirit, said Hashem, Master of Legions."[8]

Our rabbis tell us that B'nei Yisrael in Biblical Egypt merited redemption because they separated themselves from the practices of the surrounding culture in their manner of speech, dress, and by using their Jewish names, but particularly because they did not succumb in matters of morality.[9]

We will not save ourselves with armies; we will save ourselves by closeness to Hashem, the King of the Universe. *"Eleh va'rechev v'eleh va'susim*...Some [rely on] horses and some [on] chariots, but we call out in the Name of Hashem, our G-d!"[10]

The same was true in the days of Noach. For 120 years, Noach built the *teivah* in full view of the world in order that people should repent in order to avert catastrophe.

---

7   *Rashi* on *Shemos* 10:22 and 13:18.
8   *Zecharyah* 4:6.
9   *Midrash Rabbah, Parashas Emor*.
10  *Tehillim* 20:8.

> *During the 120 years [preceding the Mabul], Noach planted cedars and cut them down. "What is this for?" he was asked. "The Sovereign of the Universe has said that He will bring a flood upon the world," he replied. "If He brings a flood," they said, "He will bring it only on your house." When Mesushellach [Noach's grandfather] died, they said to [Noach], "See, the deluge has come only on your house." They mocked him, calling him "despised old man."[11]*

During the *Mabul* and in ancient Egypt, those people perished who refused to understand that their world was about to be demolished. Their civilization had seemed secure and strong; people assumed it would last forever, but it didn't.

Similarly, today, we think we are secure in a world built by the standards of Western culture.

The *Mabul* wiped out the entire world.

The *makkos* wiped out the civilization of Egypt.

Ancient Egypt was the strongest and most advanced country in the world. The borders were guarded by a charmed invisible barrier through which no person could pass.[12] Pharaoh was all-powerful; no one could defeat his army. The inhabitants were trapped inside the country like in a giant prison, similar to Communist Russia thousands of years later. Everyone was a slave. Pharaoh was considered a god. Yet, the entire civilization collapsed, and Pharaoh's army was drowned in the sea. Pharaoh was left without an army. The entire civilization crumbled and disappeared.

We have to understand why the story of ancient Egypt is so important to us Jews. Why does the Torah focus intensely on what happened there? Why does our entire holiday cycle begin with the story of *yetzias Mitzrayim*? The seminal event in Jewish history is *yetzias Mitzrayim*, as described in the Torah and in the Pesach haggadah. Every *Kiddush*

---

11 *Bereishis Rabbah* 30:7.
12 Zohar, *Parashas Bo* (37b) and *Parashas Balak* (212a), quoted in *Leil Shimurim* by Rabbi Shlomo Leib Brevda.

includes the words *"Zeicher l'yetzias Mitzrayim*—in memory of the Exodus from Egypt."

Why are we so focused on *yetzias Mitzrayim*?

Because a similar event will occur as the culminating event of history. Every word in Torah is relevant for every person, every day, forever. *"Ma'aseh Avos siman l'banim*—the events which occurred to the Avos—Avraham, Yitzchak and Yaakov—are signs for the children."[13]

The same way B'nei Yisrael were trapped as slaves in Egypt, to the extent that they believed that they were Egyptians, so today we are trapped in the worldwide Western culture that worships its own creations, its materialistic achievements, its technology, its false sense of progress, its values.

We are slaves to this culture and believe that we are part of it, and thus we are mortally endangered. Unless we open our eyes to what is happening, we are in terrible danger of going down with the surrounding culture, the same way a huge percentage of the Jews in ancient Egypt disappeared with the collapse of that seemingly invincible culture.

The hidden reason that the culture of Egypt disintegrated was in order that B'nei Yisrael should be forced to leave and become a separate and holy nation.

So too in the present world: Western culture is in danger of disintegration in order that Klal Yisrael should be saved from our immersion in that alien way of life. All the technology, the empty culture, the lack of morality, the obsession with sports and entertainment, the focus on materialism, the shopping, the obsession with eating and other pleasures…it is all going to disappear.

Just as B'nei Yisrael left Egypt in order to meet Hashem at Har Sinai and receive the Torah, so too, when today's worldwide Western culture collapses, Hashem will once again descend to the earth and give His people the Torah, as it says, "Hashem…will let us hear, in His compassion, for a second time in the presence of all the living, 'to be a G-d to you. I am Hashem, your G-d.'"[14]

---

13   *Ramban* to *Bereishis* 12:6.
14   *Kedushah* of *Shabbos Mussaf*; see *Yeshayah* 11:11.

The events of Biblical Egypt reverberated around the world, but they are going to be replayed on a vastly larger scale at the end of history. I once heard an extraordinary explanation about the wine we drink at the Pesach Seder. When we get to the part in the Haggadah that describes the *makkos*, the almost-universal custom is to dip one's finger in the wine and take out one drop of wine for each *makkah* and place the drop on our plate.

If you compare the ten drops taken out of the cup to the wine remaining in the cup, the difference is staggering. Incomparably more wine is in the cup than was taken out. This is a hint concerning the staggering difference in magnitude between *yetzias Mitzrayim* and the final redemption!

- In Egypt, B'nei Yisrael were all within one country that fell apart, but at the time of the final redemption, the entire world will be comparable to Biblical Egypt.
- In Egypt, one king fell, but in the final redemption, all the kings of the world will fall.

> *Ben Zoma [asked] the Sages: Will we mention the Exodus from Egypt in the Messianic Era? He then answers his own question: Has it not already been said, "Behold, days are coming—the word of Hashem—when people will no longer swear, 'As Hashem lives, Who brought the Children of Israel up from the Land of Egypt,' but rather, 'As Hashem lives, Who brought...back the offspring of the House of Israel from the land of the North and from all the lands wherein He had dispersed them!'"*[15]

> *[The Sages] replied: [This verse] does not [mean] that [the mentioning] of the Exodus from Egypt will be uprooted from its place [i.e., discontinued completely] but rather that [the mentioning of the redemption from] the dominion of [foreign]*

---

15   *Yirmiyah* 23:7–8.

*kingdoms will be primary, and [the mentioning of] the Exodus from Egypt will be secondary to it.*[16]

There is another remarkable commentary on the same subject: At the *Bris Bein Habesarim,* Hashem promised Avraham Avinu that he would redeem us from slavery.[17] The word referring to the punishments the Egyptians would suffer is *"dan,"* which is spelled with two letters (*"dalet"* and *"nun"*).[18] From these two letters came the many miracles and wonders of the *makkos* and *k'rias Yam Suf.* How much greater will be the redemption in the days of Moshiach, where many pages of prophecy are written in several books of the Prophets![19]

Today, the entire world is one connected culture. Even lands that were once isolated are now part of world civilization, connected by the internet and by modern means of transportation. The once-inscrutable worlds of China and Japan are now integral parts of the world trade system, intimately involved with the economic life of Western lands. Even countries that are in conflict are part of the same world culture. Muslim and Western countries, for example, are intimately connected by commerce, even if they are at war. Virtually all people today live within one giant interdependent world culture. If that culture collapses, then all within it will be affected. The only escape is to cleave to Hashem, Who is above all material existence. Just as He freed B'nei Yisrael when ancient Egypt collapsed, so He has promised to free us at the end of history.

It appears from prophetic writings that those among the other nations who cleave to Him and befriend the Jewish People will also be among those who are saved at the end of history. For example, Zecharyah HaNavi says, "And it will happen that all those who will be left from among all the nations that come upon Yerushalayim, they will ascend every year to prostrate themselves before the King, Hashem, Master of legions."[20]

---

16   *Berachos* 12b.
17   *Bereishis* 15:1ff.
18   Ibid. 15:14.
19   *Rabbeinu Yonah* on *Pirkei Avos* (1:15) quoting Rav Saadya Gaon.
20   *Zecharyah* 14:16ff; haftarah of Sukkos.

As we saw above, when that happens, instead of the world being ruled from New York, Washington, London, Paris, Berlin, Moscow, Riyadh, Teheran, Beijing, Tokyo, and so on, the world will be governed by the law of Hashem emanating from the Beis Hamikdash in Yerushalayim. As the prophet says, "*Ki miTziyon teitzei Torah u'dvar Hashem miYerushalayim*—From Tziyon will come forth Torah and the word of Hashem from Yerushalayim."[21]

At the time of the final redemption, the Jews will dwell once more in our Holy Land and the Shechinah will rest upon the Beis Hamikdash. The word of Hashem will go forth from Yerushalayim, and the entire world will live in tranquility. This could come about peacefully without tragedy or war.[22] However, as long as we Jews are enslaved to Western culture, our exile cannot end peacefully.

The passage from the *Malbim* that we saw in the previous chapter brings this out. That passage should be studied very carefully. As the reader may remember, the *Malbim* predicts a world war against the resettled modern land of Israel, followed by a mutually destructive war between the Muslims and the Western world, followed by the coming of Moshiach ben Dovid.

Many Jews have now returned to our land.

Tragically, we have not all returned to our Torah.

Without all three elements—Torah, Klal Yisrael, and the Land of Israel—our return to the land cannot be fruitful or peaceful.

The Torah tells us:

> *It will be when all these things come upon you, the blessing and the curse that I have presented before you, then you will take it to your heart among all the nations where Hashem, your G-d, has dispersed you, and you will return unto Hashem, your G-d and listen to His voice, according to everything that I command you today, you and your children, with all your heart and all your soul. Then Hashem, your G-d, will bring*

---

21  *Yeshayah* 2:3
22  See *Sanhedrin* 98a.

> back your captivity and have mercy upon you and He will return and gather you in from all the peoples to which Hashem, your G-d, has scattered you.[23]

But since so many of us have not returned spiritually, our homecoming cannot yet be successful. The modern (and secular) State of Israel was founded by people who rebelled against the Torah, and thus has been compromised from the very beginning.

> *An ox knows his owner and a donkey his master's trough, [but] Israel does not know. My people do not perceive. Woe, O sinful nation, people weighed down by iniquity, offspring of evil, destructive children; they have forsaken Hashem, they have angered the Holy One of Israel. They have turned away backwards.*[24]

Many nations throughout history were exiled from their homeland. We are the only nation—ever—to return to our homeland, as was promised in the Prophets thousands of years ago. Hashem has wrought miracles for us, and yet many Jews ignore Him.

As a result of our rebellion, we are inflamed against each other and the world is inflamed against us. Yishmael and Eisav are uniting to attack us, as the *Malbim* predicted. Frankly, it is not so difficult to understand why this is happening.

For the past two thousand years, since the destruction of the Second Temple, we have been exiled to the lands Yishmael (the Muslim culture) and Eisav (Western culture). Generally, they have rejected us, tormented us, or tortured us. There have also been exceptional periods when they acted toward us in a friendly manner, but it is not clear which is more dangerous.

It is often said that the Jews of Germany, despite constant persecution and suffering, resisted assimilation with iron strength for hundreds of years, preferring death to assimilation. But when, following the French

---

23  *Devarim* 30:1–3.
24  *Yeshayah* 1:3–4.

Revolution, the doors of the ghettos were opened and we were allowed to enter their world—that is when our strength failed. We were unable to resist the lure of the hand of friendship they seemed to offer to us, and with that hand of "friendship," we sank into the quicksand of their culture and their values.

Which is more dangerous, the kiss of Eisav or the sword of Eisav?

> *No decree against our people ever caused as much havoc as the proclamation by Napoleon of equal rights for all, and the Toleranzedict[25] of the Emperor Franz Joseph. All throughout Europe, there now began an upheaval in Jewish communities. In central and western Europe, assimilation and intermarriage became rampant. Conversion to Christianity was now a frequent phenomenon.[26]*

The last stop in our two-thousand-year exile, and perhaps the most dangerous, is America.[27] America has been very good to the Jews, but probably more Jews have been lost in the *"Goldene Medina"*[28] than anywhere else in history. The lure of American culture makes us wonder why we should be different. Why should we not partake of that "delicious banquet" the way the Jews of Shushan were drawn into the banquet prepared by Achashverosh? His banquet was even kosher!

---

25   Edict of Tolerance.
26   Rabbi Avigdor Miller, *Divine Madness*, p. 99.
27   Rabbi Chaim of Volozhin as quoted in *Mishnas R' Aron*, *chelek* 4 (speeches of Rabbi Aharon Kotler). There is a tradition, in the name of Rav Chaim of Volozhin, the prime student of the Vilna Gaon, that the last *achsanya* (inn) for the study of Torah in the exile will be America. Indeed, before Rav Avraham Jofen left Europe to come to America, he took leave of the great leader of Torah Jewry, Rav Chaim Ozer Grodzinski, who was already very sick, in the last days of his life. At the time, Rav Chaim Ozer told Rav Jofen, "I remember when I was a young boy, it was told in the name of Rav Chaim of Volozhin that the Torah will eventually be transported to America." (When Rav Chaim said this, there were hardly any Jews and certainly no yeshivas in America.) See preface to *Hamussar Vehadaas* on the Torah, from Rav Avraham Jofen. Rav Aharon Kotler is also quoted as saying, in the name of Rav Chaim of Volozhin, that the Torah will have ten *achsanyos* (inns) until Moshiach comes, and the last stop will be America. Rav Chaim cried when he said this (*Sefer Leket Reshinos*, Rav N. Wachtfogel).
28   The Golden Land, an ironic Yiddish reference to the United States.

And so today, the Jews in our world are also lured into the delicious banquet, and there we are trapped.

Now, however, since we have returned to the Land of Israel in significant numbers, and especially since we have taken upon ourselves the status of a national entity, there is a new phenomenon: the entire world has turned upon us. Both the Muslim and the Western cultures have joined hands, precisely in accordance with the words of the *Malbim*. This is consistent with the new electronic unity of the world and the creation of the United Nations, which occurred about three years before the creation of the modern State of Israel.

The United Nations was supposed to bring peace to the world. Instead, it seems that it is being used as a meeting place where the nations of the world can plot the destruction of the tiny nation of Israel. This is how the United Nations has functioned, especially in recent years. The other nations judge the State of Israel by a different standard than any other nation. It is condemned for defending itself against those who constantly attack and attempt to destroy it, and it is told what its borders should be and where its capital city should be located. No other country in the world is subjected to this treatment. In newspapers and universities around the world, Israel is constantly condemned. Thus, the *Malbim*'s prediction is borne out by current events: the world is uniting "to attack Yerushalayim."

What comes next?

"But something will go wrong with their plan."

Why should something go wrong with their plan? Why should they not succeed in destroying us and our country, G-d forbid? They outnumber us by a huge percentage.

The real question is: Why have all the empires since ancient Egypt been unable to destroy us? This brings to mind the famous quotation of Mark Twain, a non-Jew:

> *If the statistics are right, the Jews constitute but one percent of the human race. It suggests a nebulous dim puff of stardust lost in the blaze of the Milky Way. Properly the Jew ought hardly to be heard of; but he is heard of, has always been heard*

> of. He is as prominent on the planet as any other people. He has made a marvelous fight in this world, in all the ages; and he has done it with hands tied behind him...The Egyptian, the Babylonian and the Persian rose, filled the planet with sound and splendor, then faded to dreamstuff and passed away; the Greek and the Roman followed, and made a vast noise, and they are gone; other peoples have sprung up and held their torch high for a time, but it burned out, and they sit in twilight now, or have vanished. The Jew saw them all, beat them all, and is now what he always was, exhibiting no decadence, no infirmities of age, no weakening of his parts, no slowing of his energies, no dulling of his alert and aggressive mind. All things are mortal but the Jew; all other forces pass, but he remains. What is the secret of his immortality?[29]

All the empires mentioned in this passage tried to destroy us. They are all gone.

Why were they unable to destroy us?

They could not succeed because Hashem has guaranteed that the Jewish People will survive forever.

> But as for you, Yaakov, My servant, do not be afraid and do not be frightened, O Israel, for behold, I am saving you from afar, and your descendants from the land of their captivity. And Yaakov will return and be tranquil and secure, and no one will make [him] tremble. Do not be afraid, My servant Yaakov, the word of Hashem, for I am with you. Though I shall make a full end of all the nations where I have dispersed you, but of you I shall not make an end. I shall punish you with justice, but I shall not destroy you utterly.[30]

We have to take every word of the prophecy seriously.

---

29  *Harper's Magazine*, 1897.
30  *Yirmiyah* 46:27–28.

Something, therefore, *must* go wrong with the worldwide attack on Israel because Hashem has guaranteed our eternal existence. This is why we must rely on Him to protect us—because there is going to come a time when we will see that there is no other protection in the world. There will come a time when the United States does not protect us—its own Jews and those of Israel—and then we will have to realize that we have no friends in the world.

In recent years, an ominous change has come over the lands of our exile. Violence and hatred of Jews, Judaism, and the Land of Israel is increasing dramatically. The hand of our enemies is reaching out to strangle us.

There is almost certainly going to come a time—possibly very soon—when, like B'nei Yisrael at Yam Suf, we are literally surrounded and we must face the fact that we have no logical hope for survival.

What will we do then?

We will have only one place to turn.

In the words of Dovid HaMelech:

> *All the nations surround me. In the Name of Hashem I cut them down. They encircle me; they also surround me. In the Name of Hashem I cut them down. They encircle me like bees, but they are extinguished as a fire does thorns. In the Name of Hashem I cut them down.*[31]

In this chapter in *Tehillim*, Dovid HaMelech stresses one thing, and one thing only, as the formula by which we can save ourselves: calling out in the Name of Hashem. When all "logical" methods fail, we must realize there is nothing left besides Hashem.

"Hashem is close to the brokenhearted, and those crushed in spirit He saves."[32]

Listen to the words of Dovid as he faces Golyas:

---

31   *Tehillim* 118.
32   Ibid. 34.

> *Dovid said to the Philistine: "You come to me with a sword, a spear, and a javelin, but I come to you with the Name of Hashem, Master of Legions, the G-d of the battalions of Israel that you have ridiculed. On this day Hashem will deliver you into my hand. I shall smite you and remove your head from upon you, and I shall offer the carcass of the Philistine camp this day to the fowl of the heavens and to the beast of earth! Then the whole earth will know that there is a G-d in Israel, and all this assembly will know that not through sword and spear does Hashem grant salvation, for unto Hashem is the battle and He shall deliver you into our hands."*[33]

In ancient Egypt, we reached the forty-ninth level of impurity, and Hashem rescued us at the last second before we would have disappeared as a nation. We always have to hit bottom before we bounce up. "In the evening, one lies down weeping, but with dawn, a cry of joy!"[34]

When we hit bottom and the nations surround us, individual Jews may disappear. Dovid HaMelech is telling us that this is the time to call out in the Name of Hashem, which is the entire purpose of our existence in this world—to sanctify His Name.

What does it mean to sanctify Hashem's Name?

It means to tell the world that He exists and that He is the Master of the World.

Then what will happen?

The nations will surround us, either in the Land of Israel, where the hundreds of millions of descendants of Yishmael and Eisav will surround the entire land and prepare to attack us, or outside of Israel, where Jews in their communities will be surrounded.

When we wave the *arba'as haminim (lulav, esrog, hadasim and aravos)* on Sukkos, we pray for protection from six directions: north, south, east, west, up and down.

---

33  *Shmuel* I 17:45ff.
34  *Tehillim* 30.

When we are surrounded on all sides, there is only one direction to go to for protection, and that is…up! If Klal Yisrael turn to Hashem in prayer and repentance, we will be saved.

There will come a point when we realize that there is no other place to run and no other place to hide. At that time, we will turn to Hashem *"b'chol levavcha u'v'chol nafshecha u'v'chol me'odecha*—with all our heart, all our soul and everything we possess" and beg Him to save us.[35]

At that time, there will be nowhere else to turn.

Weapons will not help.

Money will not help.

Influence will not help.

Nothing will help except turning to Hashem.

> *Rabbi Yitzchak taught: In the year in which Moshiach will be revealed, all the nations of the world will be in conflict with each other. The King of Persia will quarrel with the King of Arabia, and the King of Arabia will go to the King of Aram to seek counsel from him. And the King of Persia will destroy the entire world.*
>
> *The nations will be confused and agitated and will be seized with fear and pains like the pangs of birth. Israel too will be agitated and confused, saying, "What should we do? Where shall we go?"*
>
> *Hashem will then say to them: "My children! Do not fear. All that I have done, I have done for your sake. What do you fear? Do not fear, for the time of your redemption has come! And this final redemption will not be like the first redemption [from Egypt], for the first redemption was accompanied by pain and grief and was followed by subjugation to other nations. But the final redemption will be without pain and will not be followed by subjugation to others."*[36]

---

35  *Shema* (*Devarim* 6:5).
36  *Yalkut Shimoni* (see *The Book of Our Heritage*, p. 1012).

It is possible that a nuclear war will occur in the coming years. It is very important to study the prophecy of Malachi, the last prophet, who prophesied before the destruction of the Second Temple and the beginning of our current exile. Malachi looks out over the coming two thousand years of exile. He is preparing B'nei Yisrael to survive that exile. And he tells us—giving us hope and direction—what will happen at the very end. It is essential to study his words, because we who live at this time must be prepared so that we can survive.

Here are Malachi's last prophetic words before all prophecy ended:

> *"For behold, the day is coming, burning like an oven, when all the wicked people and all the evildoers will be like straw, and that coming day will burn them up, says Hashem, Master of Legions, so that it will not leave them a root or branch. But a sun of righteousness will shine for you who fear My Name, with healing in its rays, and you will go out and flourish like calves [fattened] in the stall."*[37]

Amidst the fearful prophecy, Malachi gives us hope. There is a way out of the conflagration "for those who fear [Hashem's] Name."

This is an immeasurable source of strength.

It is possible that there will be another world war in which the entire planet is enveloped by fire, just as the entire world was enveloped by water at the time of Noach. Every thinking person is aware of this possibility, but most try to avoid thinking about it. They try to forget about it by pretending that life will go on as it has in the past.

It is understandable that people want to avoid thinking about this because it is terribly frightening to contemplate. But I believe we have no choice if we want to survive.

Another reason that people do not want to think about the oncoming cataclysm is that they do not see how they could survive it, and so they try to forget about it. They feel hopeless.

---

37  *Malachi* 3:19–20.

But Malachi says that "a sun of righteousness will shine, for you who fear My Name."

Doesn't that mean that we should work on ourselves? Doesn't that mean we should learn how to fear Hashem's Name so we can try to survive?

Fearing Hashem's Name is the way to try to save ourselves from calamity.

Malachi was prophesying to warn us and teach us what to do.

In ancient Egypt, would you have ignored Moshe, or would you have stuck close with him? It is so obvious in retrospect that the path to survival was to stick close to him! But the majority of B'nei Yisrael did not stick close to him and they perished in *Makkas Choshech*! This is suicidal behavior, but it happened. The Torah recounts it so that we can save ourselves by not following that behavior.

Similarly, with Noach, those few who were on the *teivah* survived. Obviously, Noach's behavior was sane, while the rest of the world acted insane. Even though Noach was ridiculed, he was the one who survived.

Malachi prophesied a day "burning like an oven," but we can save ourselves by understanding what is happening, returning to Hashem, and adhering to His law.

Again, let me present the words of the great rabbis of the Gemara, who instructed us about what would happen at the end of history:

"Rabbi Elazar was asked by his students: What can a person do to be spared the travails of Moshiach? [And he responded] One should occupy himself in [the study of] Torah and in acts of kindness."[38]

The rabbis have given us a path to save ourselves, the age-old path which our fathers have traveled, and that is why our holy nation exists to this day amidst the most difficult challenges ever faced by any nation. The pathway is given by Hashem.

As we leave the synagogue every morning, we say these words: "Hashem, guide me in Your righteousness, because of my watchful enemies, make Your way straight before me."[39] In other words, if we fol-

---

38   *Sanhedrin* 98b.
39   *Tehillim* 5.

low Hashem's "straight way," it will guide us safely amidst the dangers presented by our "watchful enemies."

As I pointed out above, the Gemara tells us that two things will save us in the days when the travails of Moshiach are upon the world:

- Occupying ourselves in the study of Torah
- Performing acts of kindness

One of these concerns our lifeline to the world above, and the other concerns our conduct in the world here below.

We are all aware that Torah study and acts of kindness are the cornerstones of our personal and national existence. What we are perhaps not focusing on is that they are the sole and exclusive basis for our survival.

The Western nations believe that spiritual matters are of secondary importance, for which they reserve a few hours each week, if that. The Muslim nations use spiritual ideas as their rationale for trying to destroy the world.

Both of those views are antithetical to the perspective of Klal Yisrael. As world stability becomes increasingly shaky and fragile, it is becoming clearer every moment that we must return to our roots in order to survive the imminent challenges.

Thus we focus on our unique possessions, the glory of Torah and the strength of our unity. It was only *"k'ish echad b'lev echad*—as one man with one heart"[40] that we merited to receive the Torah at Har Sinai, and it is only as one man with one heart that we will merit to receive it again, when Hashem "will let us hear, in His compassion, for a second time, in the presence of all the living…to be a G-d to you, 'I am Hashem, your G-d.'"[41]

Our challenge is so simple, yet cosmically overwhelming. The Torah is endlessly deep and infinitely high. Hashem will open our hearts and minds if we only act with love toward our brethren. Hashem will give us strength to do what seems beyond us.

---

40  *Rashi* on *Shemos* 19:2.
41  *Kedushah* of Shabbos *Mussaf* (see *Yeshayah* 11:11 and *Bamidbar* 15:41).

And so, let us go onward and try to understand how we can realize our hope to see the coming of Moshiach and the rebuilding of the Beis Hamikdash in the city of Yerushalayim.

*Chapter 4*

# THE BATTLE BETWEEN YISHMAEL AND EISAV

Let us refer again to the passage from the *Malbim*:

> *In the end of days, after Klal Yisrael have returned to their land, the children of Yishmael and the children of Eisav will unite to attack Yerushalayim. They will form a world coalition against the tiny nation of Israel. But something will go wrong with their plan. The religious beliefs of the children of Yishmael and the children of Eisav will clash, and the two nations will collide and destroy each other. This is what is referred to as the War of Gog and Magog. Following this cataclysmic conflict, the final redemption of the Jewish People will occur with the coming of Moshiach ben Dovid.*[1]

If these words are understood literally, their consequences cannot be overstressed. What does it mean, for example, that "the religious beliefs of the children of Yishmael and the children of Eisav will clash, and the two nations will collide and destroy each other?"

This is nothing less than the complete destruction of the Muslim and Western cultures as we know them! How can one contemplate the

---

1  *Malbim* on *Yechezkel* 32:17.

magnitude of these words? The only events in history to which one can compare this would be the *Mabul* or the destruction of Biblical Egypt.

> The Destruction of Edom [meaning the end of our current exile], will only come through the destruction of this world [as we know it]. The Holy One, blessed be He, will cause the very foundations of life on earth to collapse. Tranquility will be disrupted, personal lives will be filled with worry, fear, and suffering; and the entire world will cower in dread of destruction and devastation. Only then will the light of Moshiach be revealed…"and the saviors shall go up to Mount Zion to judge the mountain of Eisav."[2]

We saw an earlier phase of the war between Yishmael and Eisav on September 11, 2001, when Muslim fighters commandeered passenger airplanes and flew them deliberately into the World Trade Center and the Pentagon.

What brought about this attack?

> In the end of days, the king of the south [Yishmael] will clash with [Edom] and the king of the north. [Edom] will storm against [Yishmael] with chariots, cavalry and many ships. And he will come into many lands, flood them, and pass through them.[3]

> This [passage] refers to the final days of the last exile. The king of the south [Yishmael] will fight ferociously with Rome [Edom], as if goring him with the horn of a beast. The king of the north [Edom], also known as "Rome," will fight fiercely against him, with great force and fury, like a windstorm. He will have many great ships, and in them men of war. The king of the north [Edom] will come to the land of the king of the south [Yishmael], fight his people, and pass through there….[4]

---

2    Rabbi Eliyahu Eliezer Dessler in *Michtav Me'Eliyahu*. Rav Dessler quotes *Ovadyah* 1:21.
3    *Daniel* 11:40.
4    *Metzudas Dovid*. I saw this passage interpreting *Daniel* 11:40 in the book *Redemption*

These things are already visible in our days. The Middle East wars conducted by the United States and other Western nations in the last decades, the attack of 9/11, the worldwide growth of what is termed "terrorism," and the subsequent flood of Muslim refugees into Europe and the Americas all seem to be precise fulfillments of these prophecies and rabbinic commentaries.

It seems that the words of the *Malbim* refer not only to the Land of Israel but Jews in all lands. The *Malbim* says, "The children of Yishmael and the children of Eisav will unite to attack Yerushalayim. They will form a world coalition against the tiny nation of Israel." Over the last few years, the number of anti-Jewish attacks worldwide has been steadily increasing. In the United States, a number of Jewish centers have been attacked. In October 2018, a well-known Jewish building in Pittsburgh, Pennsylvania, was attacked by a gunman who said, "I wanted to kill Jews." Eleven people died in that attack. On the last day of Passover, about six months later, a Chabad Shul in California was attacked. There was one death and several injuries; only a miracle and the action of several courageous members, including the heroic rabbi, prevented further casualties.

As noted earlier, Dovid HaMelech writes: "All the nations surround me; in the Name of Hashem I cut them down. They encircle me, they also surround me; in the Name of Hashem I cut them down. They encircle me like bees, but they are extinguished as fire does thorns; in the Name of Hashem I cut them down."[5]

These words are interpreted by our rabbis to refer to the three-stage War of Gog and Magog.[6] The Chofetz Chaim stated that the War of Gog and Magog would be divided into three parts.[7] Note the words of the Psalm, which mentions three instances of "they surround me/ they encircle me." It is my understanding that the Chofetz Chaim referred these passages to the three phases of the War of Gog and Magog, which

---

*Unfolding*, by Rabbi A. A. Mandelbaum.
5   *Tehillim* 118.
6   *Midrash Tehillim* 109, as quoted in *Redemption Unfolding*, p. 88.
7   Ibid, pp. 90–91.

he identified as the First World War, the Second World War (which he predicted) and the final war.

- During the First World War, the centuries-old structure of Jewish settlement across Europe was destroyed.
- During the Second World War (in reference to which the corresponding language in Psalm 118 is doubled: "they encircle me; they also surround me"), the Jews were specifically singled out.
- The third passage mentions "bees," on the basis of which the Brisker Rav explained[8] that our enemies would be willing to die like bees, which seems to be a prediction of suicide bombing.[9] This passage states also that "they [will be] extinguished as fire does thorns." This also seems to relate to the prophecy of Malachi quoted previously, that, as part of the final redemption, "the day is coming, burning like an oven, when all the wicked people and all the evildoers will be like straw, and that coming day will burn them up…."

Thus, the combined attack of Yishmael and Eisav would be directed not only upon the Jews of Israel, but on Jews worldwide, and this would be the culmination of our long exile. Each time, the intensity of the attack upon Klal Yisrael becomes more focused and severe, until it is clear that the hatred of the entire world is directed against us.

The *Malbim*'s words, based on the words of Yechezkel HaNavi, tell us that Klal Yisrael will be saved from worldwide attack by the breakdown of the coalition that is attacking us, and that breakdown will grow to become the cataclysmic War of Gog and Magog in which the Muslim and Western cultures will destroy each other.

But this would be a worldwide conflict. Who could escape?

Please contemplate, my friends, the following words, which are so powerful and important that they defy description. The Chofetz Chaim is quoted as having said that the third and final war will be different

---

8   See *Redemption Unfolding*, p. 44, where it is also explained that the *gematria* of "*devorim*" (bees) is equal to the *gematria* of the words "*ben Hagar*" (son of Hagar). Hagar was the mother of Yishmael, the father of the Muslim nation.
9   Bees die after they sting.

from the first two wars. In World War I and World War II, the Angel of Death was given freedom to harm *tzaddikim* as well as evil people.

But that will not be the case in the third war.

The Chofetz Chaim is reported to have said that in the war directly before the coming of Moshiach, the Angel of Death will not have the power to harm those who cling with all their strength to Hashem and His Torah and who reject the culture of the surrounding nations.

Those who stick like glue to Hashem and His Torah will survive and go on to live in the Days of Moshiach![10]

I read a similar statement in the name of Rabbi Yechezkel Levenstein, who said, "In the final war before the coming of Moshiach, all the Jews who fear Hashem will survive. Hashem will say to them, 'All those who are removed from the secular, worldly culture…you are Mine!'"[11]

This is of cosmic significance!

Does this not give us tremendous incentive to reassess our lives?

In this scenario, only dependence upon a Power beyond nature can save us.

It is stated in Psalm 118 three times: *"B'Sheim Hashem*—In the Name of Hashem, I cut them down." This is our one and only secret of survival against all our enemies: total and explicit dependence upon Hashem. This is Dovid HaMelech's eternal message to Klal Yisrael, and this will be the message of his descendant, Moshiach ben Dovid.

It is no secret that Klal Yisrael have survived through all the centuries of our existence precisely because we depended upon a Power beyond nature to save us. Therefore, we know how to do this. The question is: Are we aware of what is happening, and are we prepared to invest all our hopes and attention, devotion and service to the King of the Universe? Are we ready to jump into the lifeboat? Are we ready to board the *teivah*?

When we hit bottom, when the abyss yawns beneath us and we see impending catastrophe before our eyes, we come to our senses and return to Hashem. This happened in Biblical Egypt, when B'nei Yisrael reached *"mem-tes shaarei tumah*—the forty-ninth level of impurity."

---

10    Heard from Rabbi Matisyahu Salomon.
11    *Leket Rishimos*, as quoted in *Redemption Unfolding*.

One more notch downward and we would have disappeared as a distinct and holy nation. From that dangerous place, Moshe Rabbeinu took us out of slavery—to Har Sinai and eternal freedom through allegiance to the Master of the Universe.

But not everyone followed Moshe Rabbeinu. The inescapable conclusion is that everything, our entire future in this world and the next, depends entirely on our allegiance to the Torah. When we deviate, G-d forbid, then Hashem sends enemies to bring us back to our senses. As we say every day in the *Shema*:

> *Beware lest your heart be seduced and you turn astray and serve gods of others and bow to them. Then the wrath of Hashem will blaze against you. He will restrain the heaven so there will be no rain and the ground will not yield its produce. And you will swiftly be banished from the goodly land which Hashem gives you.*[12]

Here is a *pasuk* from the haftarah we read on Shabbos Chol Hamoed *Sukkos:* "Every man's sword shall be against his brother."[13]

I had assumed this meant that Jews would be fighting Jews, which seemed to make no sense. But then I saw a comment by Rabbi Don Isaac Abarbanel, who writes that these words allude to "Edom and Yishmael, for they are brothers through their original forefathers." In other words, this is a prophecy that Edom (Eisav's descendants) and Yishmael's descendants will fight each other in the days before the final redemption. The *Abarbanel* writes that this war will be so powerful and the fear will be so great that everyone will flee as if there were a great earthquake, and that this is what the prophet Zecharyah refers to when he writes that the Mount of Olives will split.[14] Why do Yishmael and Eisav hate each other?

Here is a way of explaining by examining the Western, Muslim, and—*lehavdil*—Jewish calendars.

---

12   *Devarim* 11:16–17.
13   *Yechezkel* 38:21.
14   *Zecharyah* 1:12.

The Western calendar is based on the sun, specifically the amount of time it takes for the earth to make one revolution around the sun.

Western culture reflects the nature of its calendar, because the descendants of Edom, who comprise the inhabitants of the Western world, are culturally aligned to the sun. It is a "daytime" culture, whose members work "under the sun."[15] Rome, the progenitor of Western culture, was a culture whose hallmark was its great materialistic achievements: the construction of roads, viaducts, ships, and instruments of war and destruction, like the catapult. The civilization that descended from Rome, the Western world (from which came the Church of Rome and its "offspring"), prides itself on its material accomplishments: "taming the wilderness" and building roads, bridges, skyscrapers (including the World Trade Center, which was destroyed by Yishmael in 2001), cars, airplanes, rockets, traditional and nuclear weapons, computers, the internet, and all the offshoots of technology. All these are the products of a civilization that is focused on material accomplishments, which are constructed during daylight hours, "under the sun." Night is for relaxation, so that one can return refreshed to the next day's work.

The Muslim calendar is the opposite of the Western calendar. It is based on the moon. Its months are totally tied to the moon. As a result, they "wander" around through the solar year. Ramadan, for example, can occur at any season of the year because the months are not tied to a particular season the way they are in the Western calendar.

Fascinatingly, the Islamic culture reflects this. They are not builders. They are actually, by nature, destroyers. As the Torah tells us, Yishmael, the progenitor of the Muslim culture, is described as "a wild-ass of a man. His hand [will be] against everyone and everyone's hand [will be] against him...."[16] Yishmael's descendants are by nature stealthy nomads, living in the shifting sands of the desert, quick with the sword and knife, and often operating in darkness. Their symbol, unsurprisingly, is the moon, under whose influence they move, in darkness.

---

15    *Koheles* 1:3 and many other passages in *Koheles*.
16    *Bereishis* 16:12.

To sum up: Yishmael's descendants go stealthily under the moon. Edom's descendants work under the sun.

Are these the only two calendar systems in the world? Not at all.

The Jewish calendar is amazingly similar to yet amazingly different from both the Muslim and Western calendars, and it demonstrates how Am Yisrael is a unique nation, whose very basis far surpasses the nature of any other nation on earth.

The Muslim and Western calendars are subservient to the sun and moon, the "luminaries that Hashem created,"[17] but Am Yisrael is above all creation and our calendar is mandated not by subservience to the world of nature, but—since it originates in the Torah—it is by definition above all of nature.

Those who adhere to this calendar can actually soar above nature. As the Torah attests, Hashem "took [Avram] outside,"[18] to which *Rashi* says, "[Hashem] took [Avram] out of the space of the world and raised him above the stars."[19]

The *chiddush* in the Jewish calendar is that it is based on both the sun and the moon! The months are lunar, but they are prevented from "wandering" around the seasons (as they do in the Muslim calendar) by the fact that the month of *Nissan* must occur within a certain time period around the spring equinox[20] (usually March 20 in the Western calendar, on which the day and night are of equal duration). As the *pasuk* says, "in the month of *Aviv*."[21]

"The Torah requires that [the month of] *Nissan* be '*chodesh ha'aviv*,' the month of springtime."[22] Thus the lunar months are tied to the solar cycle, and the Jewish calendar differs fundamentally from both the Muslim and Western calendars. As I stated above, instead of being subservient to the heavenly bodies like other nations, we are above nature by virtue of the fact that our lifestyle is regulated by the Torah.

---

17  *"Keil Adon,"* which we say Shabbos morning.
18  *Bereishis* 15:3.
19  *Bereishis Rabbah* 44:12.
20  To accomplish this, an extra month is inserted during seven years of each nineteen-year cycle.
21  *Devarim* 16:1.
22  Artscroll commentary on *Shemos* 12:2, *Stone Chumash*.

Other nations have tried to copy us. They take one part of our system or another part of our system, but the synthesis of moon and sun, spiritual and material that is uniquely ours, they can neither understand nor can they live by. That is how we are able to exist both in the material and the spiritual world. Like Yaakov's ladder, our feet are on the ground, but our head is in Heaven.

Those who dwell to an excessive degree in the material world or the spiritual world live an extreme and unbalanced existence, but we combine, incorporate, and harmonize both the material and the spiritual, the temporal and the eternal. We are high, but we are also deep. In the material world of history, we wax and wane like the moon, but in the spiritual world, our flame burns steadily like the light of the sun. We have a balance that is shared by no other nation. Our calendar tells the story.

As we know from Chazal, Hashem created the sun and the moon of equal size, but the moon complained to Hashem, "It is impossible for two kings to use the same crown." Hashem then "punished" the moon for its contentiousness and jealousy by reducing its size.[23]

This sounds like a fairy tale, but it is no fairy tale at all.

In fact, this "fairy tale" explains the history of the past fourteen hundred years.

We have just said that the sun is associated with Eisav/Rome, and the moon with Yishmael/Islam. This helps explain a quandary I contemplated for years: Why does Islam constantly attack the descendants of Eisav?

What, for example, is the origin of the events of September 11, 2001? Why have the two cultures been fighting ever since Islam was created some fourteen hundred years ago? We know that Islam demands that the entire world adhere to its belief; one who refuses is deserving of death. That is the origin of "Jihad," the so-called holy war. Islam has always tried—sometimes with greater and sometimes with lesser

---

23   *Chullin* 60b; *Rashi* on *Bereishis* 1:16.

success—to take over the world. Islam and the Roman world have been jockeying back and forth for centuries.

How do we explain it? What do they have against each other? If you go back to their origins, isn't Yishmael really fighting Yitzchak and Eisav fighting Yaakov? Yes, that is true, but why are they fighting each other?

This made no sense to me until I remembered how these two nations resemble the sun and the moon. And then I remembered that the moon attacked the sun in the beginning of time. And why are they fighting? Here again is what *Rashi* says: "The [two] great lights...were created equal and the moon was reduced because it complained and said, 'It is impossible for two kings to use the same crown.'"[24] The moon wanted to rule the world and so it attacked the sun. On September 11, the moon attacked the sun.

Now perhaps we can understand the conflict between Yishmael and Eisav. They are jealous of each other, but Israel is, *lehavdil*, "*samei'ach b'chelko*—[We are] satisfied with our lot."[25]

On that basis, we can try to understand the origin of this primordial conflict and the mechanism by which the War of Gog and Magog may begin.

Read what the prophet Ovadyah writes about Eisav/Edom:

> *Behold, on that day—the word of Hashem—I will eradicate wise men from Edom and understanding from the mountain of Eisav....For the oppression of your brother Yaakov, disgrace will envelop you and you will be cut off forever....You should not have entered the gate of My people on the day of their disaster; you should not have gazed upon its misfortune on the day of its disaster; you should not have put your hands on its wealth on the day of its disaster! You should not have stood at the crossroads to cut down its refugees; you should not have imprisoned its survivors on the day of distress.... For the day of Hashem upon all the nations is near; as you did, so will be*

---

24  *Rashi* on *Bereishis* 1:16.
25  *Pirkei Avos* 4:1.

> *done to you, your recompense shall return upon your head.... The house of Yaakov will be a fire and the house of Yosef a flame—and the house of Eisav like straw, and they will ignite them and devour them.... Saviors will ascend Mount Tziyon to judge the mountain of Eisav, and the kingdom will be Hashem's.*[26]

The prophets predict an utter end to Eisav at the end of history. But Eisav will not be alone. The *Malbim* says that Yishmael will be the instrument that destroys Eisav. In that process, Yishmael will also be destroyed.

One must take a deep breath to contemplate this, because we are speaking about the complete overturning of world culture, the culture in which we live and which has ruled the world for two thousand years. We do not know what form this will take. It is possible, if Klal Yisrael return in repentance, that the process could be peaceful, but it is clear that we are speaking about events that are too vast to comprehend.

The world today seems so flammable and dangerous that one can imagine a scenario of destruction on a worldwide scale. It would coincide with the words of the *Malbim*, which in turn are based on the prophetic words of Yechezkel. It is also consistent with the words of Malachi, who said, "Behold, the day is coming, burning like an oven...."

Eisav are builders by nature; Yishmael are destroyers by nature. Those who destroyed the World Trade Center are ready to destroy again. The dry tinder is there, ready to be ignited. All that is missing is the match to light the fuse.

Right now, Western society is extremely vulnerable.

Behavioral standards have reached a point that could cause society to collapse even without external enemies. Immoral behavior is now established as law in many Western lands, which are actually trying to make moral behavior illegal. The United States Supreme Court, for example, has given the force of law to behavior that is described in the Torah as "abomination." As we discussed earlier, the *Mabul* was unleashed upon

---

26   *Ovadyah* 1:8ff.

the world because immorality and robbery became rampant, signifying a worldwide rebellion against Hashem.

Through its encouragement of immorality, it follows that Western culture has lost the moral basis for its existence. As a result, the fabric of unity that any society needs to stay together is unraveling. Unless there is repentance and a return to moral standards of behavior, which seems unlikely, it is hard to understand how Western culture can survive. If Western culture collapses, mass chaos would almost certainly overwhelm mankind throughout this beleaguered planet.

> *The degraded man says in his heart, "There is no Hashem." They have corrupted and made abominable their actions. There is no doer of good. From heaven Hashem gazed down upon mankind, to see if there exists a reflective person who seeks out Hashem. Everyone has gone astray. Together they have become depraved. There is no doer of good. There is not even one....*[27]

Corruption in our generation is reaching catastrophic proportions.

I want to quote here a remarkable passage written by the late Rabbi Shlomo Lorincz:

> *When I visited America, I met the [former] President of the United States, Harry Truman, in his hometown of Kansas City, with Rabbi Solomon, one of the rabbis of the city.*
>
> *President Truman said to me, "I am happy to have the opportunity to explain to the rabbi why I recognized the State of Israel, something that was [apparently] against the interests of the United States, to favor 650,000 Jews who wanted their own country, where around that country you have tens of millions of Arabs who are against it. As is known, in the city where I grew up, one of the newspapers came out with a headline, 'Truman the Traitor.'"*

---

27  *Tehillim* 14.

He continued his interesting monologue: *"In my youth, I grew up in a neighborhood of Jewish families whom I looked up to. On the Sabbath I would turn on and off the lights for one of the Jewish families, and, as a reward, I got a slice of bread. My father's custom was to read the Bible to me every Sunday. When we read about Koresh, the King of Persia, who gave the Jews permission to return to the Land of Judah and to build the Temple in Jerusalem, I thought to myself that a day will come when I will be the President of the United States—the dream of every child in America was to be the president—I am going to do what King Koresh did in his time.*

*"The dream came to fruition, and when your president, Chaim Weitzman, came to me—and in his hand was a gift, a Torah scroll—and he asked that I give the United Nations representative instructions to support your country, I remembered everything that was in my heart in my youth.*

*"It was clear [however,] that these feelings from the memory of my youth could not weigh against the responsibilities and interests of the United States, so why—with all this—did I come out for your side, on your behalf, and recognize the State of Israel?*

*"The reason for this is that only Stalin and I knew the true dangers that faced the world. (This was just after the Hiroshima bombing.) The possibility of an atomic war will continue to threaten to destroy the world, and—even more—to leave the residents of the world in a situation worse than death.*

*"And if I still have the will to continue to live, it is only because I believe that, just like in the past, three thousand years ago, you Jews saved humanity, wild mankind, via your Torah, so too I believe and hope that, even nowadays, you, the Jewish Nation, will be successful again, to enlighten and to heal the beasts of cruelty in our midst and save the world from total destruction."*

> *When I returned to Israel from that interesting meeting, I gave over the words of President Truman from the podium of the Knesset, so that the leaders should know what the leaders of the world expect of the Jewish Nation. These words are copied in the archives of the speeches of the Knesset.*
>
> *The wise among the nations know that the job of the Jewish Nation is to be a light unto the nations, and through the Torah that is in our hands to save the world from destruction and to cause goodness to come to the world. If we don't actualize this mission, our friends will turn their backs on us and they will conduct themselves solely focused on their own interests, and then they will favor the hundred million Arabs and the billion Muslims over the handful of Jews.*
>
> *Our obligation is to ensure that Hashem's Name is great and sanctified, and then we will merit that Hashem will fulfill His promise, and our problems will find the best solution [until the day of Moshiach].*[28]

President Truman was correct. We, Klal Yisrael, have the power to save the world from destruction.

---

28 From the introduction to the book *Miluai Shlomo* by Rabbi Shlomo Lorincz. (I am grateful to Rabbi Yechezkel Shraga Weinfeld for showing me this fascinating passage.)

*Chapter 5*

# SURVIVAL THROUGH TORAH

It is axiomatic that we survive through Torah.

Torah is equivalent to all the mitzvos. As our rabbis tell us, *"Talmud Torah k'neged kulam*—Talmud Torah is equivalent to them all."[1] That makes perfect sense, because Torah is the source for all the mitzvos and how to perform them.

Torah makes Am Yisrael unique. Hashem did not speak to any other nation, nor did He give His law to any other nation.

Am I saying anything new?

Nothing.

So why am I writing this?

Because there is something wrong, and we are not getting it.

Let me recapitulate what we have said up until now.

Moshiach is not here yet. As long as Moshiach is not here, we are not where we are supposed to be. And right now, we are in terrible danger.

Attacks against Jews are becoming epidemic throughout the world, both inside and outside the Land of Israel. For a few years after the Holocaust, hatred against Jews was considered inappropriate in the "civilized" world, but lately the nations have forgotten their positive feelings, the way Pharaoh's butler quickly forgot about Yosef, and then, later, Pharaoh himself forgot about Yosef.

---

1   *Maseches Shabbos* 127a.

Rabbi Yaakov Feitman wrote the following, referring to the "ancient question" of why Pharaoh himself did not expel the Jews from Egypt. Why did he not simply let them go?[2]

> *If the redemption from Egypt would have come about…with Pharaoh playing the role of the "Great Emancipator"…this would have created a situation where the Jewish nation would be eternally indebted to Pharaoh [and not Hashem] for granting them independence by permitting them to leave Egypt.*[3]

Rabbi Feitman then quotes Rav Avrohom Pam, who extrapolates on this theme in relation to the final redemption:

> *This idea explains the purpose of the United Nations organization…in Hashem's grand scheme to bring the world to its ultimate fulfillment. The U.N. accomplishes very little and is virtually powerless…. What is its purpose? Perhaps the answer is, as the Gemara says, that when the end of days will arrive…the nations will come before Hashem and demand reward for all the good they had done for the Jewish nation. Each will describe how it built projects to make life easier for Israel, [but] Hashem will "seal their mouths" and show them how everything they did was for their own benefit, to make money and to indulge in worldly pleasures, with the thought of helping the Jewish nation the farthest from their true intentions….*
>
> *The purpose of the United Nations in Hashem's plan is to serve as a permanent unimpeachable record of the hatred of the nations for Am Yisrael. Every speech is recorded. The tallies of every anti-Israel vote and resolution are documented. All the fiery condemnations by the Arab, Soviet, and Third*

---

2   See, for example, *Shemos* 1:9 where Pharaoh states to "his people" that B'nei Yisrael were becoming a potential danger to Egypt.
3   *Yated Ne'eman*, January 2017.

> World blocs and the deafening response of total silence by the others will serve as clear, indisputable evidence of the true feelings of the world toward Israel and the Jews.
>
> What other purpose can there be for this do-nothing organization?.... This realization should be a source of great consolation to us in trying to understand the happenings of our troubled times.[4]
>
> Bilaam, although a vicious enemy, was forced by Hashem to speak the truth about B'nei Yisrael: "Behold, it is a nation that will dwell in solitude and not be reckoned among the nations."[5]

The Torah describes the Biblical prototype to our exile. In Egypt our danger reached a terrible climax, at which either we or Egypt had to give way.

So it seems for us in today's world. We are reaching a point at which the entire world will unite to destroy us and there will be nowhere to hide. At that moment, there will likely be a cosmic change in the world. Either we, G-d forbid, or our enemies will be destroyed. But since Hashem promises us that we will never be completely destroyed, we know which way the drama of history will turn out.

> But you, do not be afraid, My servant Yaakov, and do not be frightened, Oh Israel, for I shall save you from afar, and your offspring from the land of their captivity, and Yaakov shall return and be tranquil...and none shall make him tremble. You, do not be afraid, My servant Yaakov—the words of Hashem—for I am with you. Though I shall make an end of all the nations where I have scattered you, of you I shall not make an end. I shall punish you with justice, but I shall not destroy you utterly.[6]

---

4    *Shabbos with Rav Pam, Parashas Bo.*
5    *Bamidbar* 23:9.
6    *Yirmiyah* 46:27.

The objective is to survive "*chevlei Moshiach*—the birth pangs of Moshiach" and live to see the perfect world that awaits those who are loyal to the Master of the Universe.

As Dovid HaMelech says, "*Lu ami shome'a li*—If only My people would heed Me, if Israel would walk in My ways, in a moment I would subdue their foes."[7] But we do not take Hashem's words seriously, because of the dust of exile swirling around us. This is what happened in Biblical Egypt. As it says: "Moshe spoke…to B'nei Yisrael, but they did not heed Moshe because of shortness of breath and hard work."[8]

The *Ohr Hachaim* explains: "Perhaps it is because [B'nei Yisrael] were not attached to the Torah that they did not listen, and that deficiency is called 'shortness of breath,' for the Torah expands the heart of a person."[9]

Rabbi Samson Raphael Hirsch says:

> *The inhumanity of the present weighed heavily [on B'nei Yisrael], and the need to meet its demands and to find for themselves even a momentary respite sapped all their strength. They were drained of all spirit and did not have the energy to turn their thoughts to the future, of which Moshe wished to speak to them. They were so pressed by the demands of the present and so burdened by their work that they did not even have the patience to listen to him quietly.*[10]

Today, our foes are multiplying, but we have to know that the climactic moment is near. As Dovid HaMelech says, "When the wicked bloom like grass and all the doers of iniquity blossom, it is only to destroy them to eternity."[11]

The central question is: How will we survive until then?

---

7  *Tehillim* 81.
8  *Shemos* 6:9.
9  *Ohr Hachaim* on *Shemos* 6:9.
10 Rabbi Samson Raphael Hirsch on *Shemos* 6:9.
11 *Tehillim* 92.

The *Gemara* asks: "What can a person do to be spared the travail of Moshiach?" And the Gemara answers: "One should occupy himself in [the study of] Torah and acts of kindness."[12]

Rabbi Chaim of Volozhin describes the effect of Torah learning upon the world:[13]

> *The world continues to exist in the merit of the few remaining Torah scholars who learn day and night. [It is due to their Torah study] that the world is not destroyed and returned to primeval emptiness and void.... When people stop learning Torah, the Holy One, blessed be He, seeks to destroy the world. Furthermore, it says... "Every day, destructive angels go forth from before Hashem to wipe out the entire world. If not for the synagogues and study halls where Torah scholars are sitting and learning, the destructive angels would instantly annihilate the entire world."[14] The Gemara says, "The person who studies Torah for its own sake provides protection for the whole world."[15] And the Mishnah says, "The creation of the whole world is worthwhile for [the Torah scholar's] sake alone."[16]*

"Rabbi Abba bar Kahana said: All of [Bilaam's blessings] were eventually transformed into the curse [he had intended], except for the [curse regarding] synagogues and study houses...."[17] If Hashem had not been merciful and He had allowed all of Bilaam's curses to take effect, then we would not exist today, G-d forbid! But our synagogues and study houses, where we pray and study Torah, were protected, and therefore, through them alone we have survived!

Torah is the sole basis of our survival.[18]

---

12 *Sanhedrin* 98b.
13 *Nefesh Hachaim*, gate 4, chap. 25.
14 *Eliyahu Rabbah*.
15 *Sanhedrin* 99b.
16 *Avos* 6:1.
17 *Sanhedrin* 105b.
18 Acts of kindness and Torah go together because we received the Torah at Har Sinai only

How is it that the study of Torah and acts of kindness are the keys that unlock the door to the perfect world that awaits those who are loyal to the King of the Universe?

The Chofetz Chaim would say, "The evil inclination does not mind if a Jew fasts, weeps, and prays all day long, provided he does not study Torah!"[19] Nothing disturbs the *yetzer hara* like Torah study. This, above all, is what he wants to prevent.

Why is Torah study the supreme object of the Satan's attention? Obviously, if our principal enemy, whose entire "occupation" is to damage us, wants to keep us away from Torah, then Torah must be supremely important. What is it about Torah study that is of such importance that the Satan himself is—so to speak—obsessed with it?

The Gemara lists ten mitzvos "whose fruits a person enjoys in this world but whose principal remains intact for him in the World to Come." Of those ten, "the study of Torah is equivalent to them all."[20]

It is said that Hitler, *yemach shemo*, wanted above all to rid the world of the "*Shas Yidden*," the *talmidei chachamim*, the Jews who study Torah "*yomam va'layla—day and night*." Even—or perhaps especially—our most bitter enemies are aware of this central, most important aspect of the life of the Jew.

And what are they really after?

Dovid HaMelech describes it: "Remember, Hashem, for the offspring of Edom, the Day of Yerushalayim—for those who say 'Destroy! Destroy! To its very foundation.'"[21]

This is what they are after. They want to eliminate the very core of our existence, G-d forbid. They want to eliminate us from the world down to the very last individual—G-d forbid!—so that a Jew will never again appear in the world until the end of time.

And why?

They are really after Hashem.

---

by virtue of the fact that we were united as "one man with one heart," and this is based on *chessed*, kindness, the unity of Am Yisrael.
19  Artscroll *Bereishis*, overview to *Vayishlach*, p. 1400.
20  *Maseches Shabbos* 127a.
21  *Tehillim* 137.

They want Hashem to leave them alone. They know He exists, but they want Him to remain in Heaven and not bother them here on earth so that they can pursue their egotistic, voracious, violent, lewd lifestyles without anyone telling them it is not permissible!

It is like Eisav saying to Yaakov, "Pour into me, now, some of that red, red stuff!"[22] They want to stuff it all down their throats…now! They are like the generation of *migdal Bavel*, who tried to fight Hashem and tell Him to keep out of their lives.

And we, the Jewish People, are the chosen ones of Hashem, who represent Him in this world through the Torah that He gave to us. We are the targets of the evil nations who still—to this day—want the world to be left alone, and they want the Master of the Universe to disappear.

But since He will not go away nor will He disappear, they want His representatives in the world to disappear, G-d forbid.

And so they aim their attack on us, the *"Torah Yidden,"* the Jews who study the holy Torah day and night and who bring the sanctity of Heaven into this world, who bring morality and peace into the world, who hate bloodshed and gluttony and promiscuity.

Israel, particularly Yerushalayim, and especially Har Habayis are their targets for one reason, which is strikingly clear: because Har Habayis, the seat of the Beis Hamikdash, is the location from which Torah goes forth to the world, and our enemies hate Torah.

As we say on Tishah B'Av, "Oh, most desirable land, you have been placed in the center of all nations, and from Eden, the source of all splendor, your rivers emanated."[23]

> *Eretz Yisrael is positioned in the center of the world: Yerushalayim is at the center of Eretz Yisrael; the Temple is at the center of Yerushalayim; the Heichal Hall is at the center of the Temple, and the Holy Ark is at the center of the Heichal.*[24]

This is the most coveted place in the entire world.

---

22   *Bereishis* 25:30.
23   *Kinnah* 37.
24   *Midrash Tanchuma*, *Kedoshim* 10, as quoted in the Artscroll Tishah B'Av Siddur, pp. 332–33.

Our enemies, the children of Yishmael, have built their mosque right on top of the *"even shesiyah,"*[25] the location of the *Aron* that contained the *Luchos* that Hashem gave to Moshe Rabbeinu on Har Sinai. This is the place from which the Torah goes forth to the world, and Yishmael have been sitting on that spot for hundreds of years just to keep us and our Torah far away—so they can try to live as they please without restraint from the King of the Universe.

In the days of Chanukah, the Greeks who ruled the Land of Israel wanted above all to separate us from the Torah. As our rabbis have written, "In the days of Matisyahu, the son of Yochanan, the High Priest, the Hasmonean, and his sons, when the wicked Greek kingdom rose up against Your people, Israel, to make them forget Your Torah and compel then to stray from the statutes of Your will…."[26]

One of the most famous scenes in the Torah is the battle between Yaakov Avinu and the angel of Eisav. As it says, "A man battled with [Yaakov] the entire night." This "man" is an angel who, our rabbis tell us, is the Heavenly protector of Eisav. Each nation has its own guardian angel.

Each of the Avos is said to represent a different aspect of Torah. Avraham Avinu represents kindness. He is the one who opened his tent to everyone and, through his *chessed* and fearless truth-telling, taught the entire world that Hashem exists.

Yitzchak Avinu represents strength and service. It was he who was willing to sacrifice his life to sanctify Hashem's Name at the *Akeidah*, the "binding of Yitzchak."

Yaakov Avinu represents Torah.[27] The Torah says, "Yaakov was a wholesome man, abiding in tents."[28] *Rashi* explains that "tents" refers to the study hall.

Where did Yaakov Avinu study? Adam, the first man, had a son whose name was Sheis. Sheis founded a yeshiva. As it says in the Zohar, "Adam

---

25 The foundation stone, the place from which the rest of the world was built. This is the place on which the *Aron* rested in the Beis Hamikdash (*Yoma* 54b).
26 Chanukah *tefillah*, inserted into *Shemoneh Esreh* and *bentching*.
27 See Artscroll *Bereishis*, overview to *Vayishlach*, p. 1400.
28 *Bereishis* 25:27.

knew the Torah, and he transmitted it to Sheis."[29] Yaakov, of all the Avos, is recognized as being identified with the study of Torah.

What does this have to do with Yaakov battling an angel?

That angel represents the enemies of Torah. Eisav, whose war with his twin brother Yaakov has lasted until this very day, tried to bring about Yaakov's downfall by striking against his very essence, which is Torah. The angel was trying to separate Yaakov's descendants from Torah. And who are Yaakov's descendants? We are, the Children of Israel, the Jews of today!

The essence of our nation is Torah. "It is a tree of life for those who grasp it, and its supporters are praiseworthy. Its ways are ways of pleasantness and all its paths are peace....Hashem desired, for the sake of [Israel's] righteousness, that the Torah be made great and glorious."[30]

The scene in which Eisav's angel battles with Yaakov foreshadows the battle down through the coming millennia in which the nations of the world attempt to destroy the essence of Israel. It is repeated in every generation up to this very day. As we say on Seder night, "*Shebechol dor va'dor*...In every generation there are those who rise against us to annihilate us...."[31] This will not cease until the "break of dawn," the moment in which Moshiach comes, when the power of our enemies is broken forever.

> *Yaakov was left alone and a man wrestled with him until the break of dawn. When [the angel] perceived that he could not overcome [Yaakov], he struck the socket of his hip, so Yaakov's hip-socket was dislocated as he wrestled with him. Then [the angel] said, "Let me go, for dawn has broken." And [Yaakov] said, "I will not let you go unless you bless me." [The angel] said to him, "What is your name?" He replied, "Yaakov." [The angel] said, "No longer will it be said that your name is 'Yaakov,' but 'Israel,' for you have striven with the Divine and with man*

---

29　*Zohar Chadash* 22b.
30　*Shacharis*, based on *Mishlei* and *Yeshayah*.
31　Haggadah.

> *and [you] have overcome." Then Yaakov…said, "Divulge, if you please, your name." And [the angel] said, "Why then do you inquire of my name?" And [the angel] blessed [Yaakov] there. So Yaakov called the name of the place Peniel, "For I have seen the Divine face to face, yet my life was spared."*[32]

One reason, our rabbis tell us, that the angel of Eisav refused to divulge his name is that he constantly changes identity, attempting to fool us by appearing in different guises. Sometimes he appears disguised as a great Torah scholar, sometimes as an obvious enemy, and otherwise everything in between. Truly, he is an adversary against whom we need the most powerful weapon, and the only weapon sufficiently powerful is the Torah itself.

Hashem says, "I have created the evil inclination [and] I have created Torah as its antidote."[33]

All our troubles come about as a result of abandoning the Torah.

> *Why was the land [of Israel] destroyed, left desolate as a desert without passersby? Hashem said, "Because they forsook My Torah."*[34] *We find that the Holy One, blessed be He, overlooked idolatry, adultery, and bloodshed, but He would not overlook the debasement of Torah…[Hashem says] if only they had forsaken Me but observed [the study of] My Torah…. For if they had observed My Torah, as a result of having involved themselves with it, it would have brought them back to Me."*[35]

The *yetzer hara* especially tries to prevent us from learning Torah. This challenge exists with all mitzvos, but the greatest challenge is Torah study. Sometimes, we feel the resistance as soon as we start just *thinking* about Torah study! Our minds come up with countless other things that "must" be done before we begin to learn.

---

32   *Bereishis* 32:25–31.
33   *Kiddushin* 30b.
34   *Yirmiyah* 9:11–12.
35   *Yalkut Shemoni*, as quoted in Artscroll *Bereishis*, pp. 1398–9.

All this, despite the fact that we know with absolute certainty that Torah study is what enables us—and the entire world—to survive!

It is written that if there were no Jew studying Torah at a particular time anywhere in the world, the world would at that moment cease to exist. It is a fact that, somewhere in the world, at every moment, there are always Jews studying Torah, and so the world continues to exist. In the words of Rabbi Chaim Volozhin: "Unquestionably…if there would be one moment when not one person is engrossed in Torah study somewhere in the entire world, all the upper and lower worlds would instantly cease to exist, G-d forbid."[36]

> Why are [Torah scholars] compared to pillars? Because they…hold up the world. As it says: "If My covenant…would not be, [it would have been as if] I had not set up the laws of heaven and earth." Says the Holy One, blessed be He, "When someone learns Torah and wisdom, I consider it as if he had created the heaven and established the entire world." And the Zohar says: "Whoever immerses himself in the Torah every day will have a share in the World to Come and will be considered as if he had built worlds, because the world is founded on the Torah…. Hashem created the world with the breath of His mouth, and through the breath of those who learn Torah the world endures…. Hashem looked into the Torah and created the world. Man looks into the Torah and upholds the world."[37]

If a Jew studying Torah is so powerful that his Torah study is the sole determining factor in whether or not the world continues to exist, how is it that we often have such a powerful resistance to studying Torah? How could anyone run away from Torah?

That, my friends, is the work of the *yetzer hara*, the angel of Eisav. He is not just fighting Yaakov, but he is fighting all of Yaakov's children every second, trying to separate us from Torah, G-d forbid, so that he can destroy the world. That is the eternal struggle…until Moshiach comes!

---

36   *Nefesh Hachaim*, gate 4, ch. 11.
37   Ibid.

This struggle is for our personal existence and the continued existence of the world. Satan, as we said, has many names, including the Angel of Death and the *yetzer hara*. As the Gemara states, "Satan, the *yetzer hara*, and the Angel of Death are one and the same."[38]

The *yetzer hara* does not want to divulge his name because identifying him is in itself a weapon against him. His very identity is that he has no identity. He is, in essence, a force of destruction. The epitome of non-existence exists only to destroy that which exists, and all that stands between him and the achievement of his goal are the Jews who study Torah.

We can begin to see what is going on—the antagonism we sometimes feel toward Torah study is the Satan fighting within us!

The Torah is the work of the living Hashem. The *yetzer hara* tells us that to be ruled by Hashem is the worst kind of slavery, the most restricted lifestyle, worse than nothing.

But we have a choice.

Before we are born, while we are in our mother's womb, an angel comes to teach us the entire Torah.[39] When we are born, the angel hits us on the mouth. That is the shock of birth. With that shock, we forget everything the angel had taught us. As we travel through life, we absorb endless bits of information.

If, however, we are fortunate enough to learn Torah, it sounds familiar to us because we have heard those words before. That is when we remember the words the angel spoke to us inside our mother's womb.

Thus Torah is familiar to us because we learned it from the angel!

That means that people who reject Torah also know Torah. This in fact is exactly what they are running away from! They know the Torah and, because they know that it entails complete subservience to the Master of the Universe, they run away from it. They are trying to rebel against Him, like Adam and Chavah in Gan Eden, and all since then who have followed the desires of their heart rather than the voice of Hashem.

---

38   *Bava Basra* 16a.
39   *Niddah* 30b.

Like the generation of *migdal Bavel*, they want to battle Hashem and "force" Him to leave His own world, the world that He created.

> The woodworker stretches a line and marks [the wood] with chalk. He works on it with planes and marks it with a compass. He makes it like a man's form, like human splendor, to stay inside a house. Cutting cedars for it, he takes laurel and oak and reinforces it with trees of the forest. He plants a fir tree and the rain makes it grow. It will be fuel for man. He will take from it and warm himself, or even kindle a fire and bake bread. Yet he also makes a god and prostrates himself. He makes it a graven idol and bows [to it]. He burns half of it in fire, or with half [he prepares] meat to eat, roasting it and sating himself, or he warms himself and says, "Ah, I have warmed myself. I see the flame." Then the rest of it he makes into a god as his graven image. He will bow to it and prostrate himself and pray to it, and say, "Rescue me, for you are my god."[40]

This is how the world fools itself!

Because everyone knows Torah from the womb, for precisely that reason do we run away from it. We know it is true and we are afraid of it. We attempt to assume control of our life and keep Hashem out of the picture.

People pretend that their own manufactured "god" is Hashem. It's like the apartment houses that label the thirteenth floor "fourteen." People pretend that night is day, black is white, or left is right.

Because they know the Torah is true, they then—to rationalize their rebellion—must mock and demonize those who follow the Torah. This is why there are Jews who are the worst anti-Semites, because they know in their soul that their lives are lies. In order to rationalize their lifestyle, they must tell themselves that those who follow Hashem are fools or hypocrites or liars or thieves.

---

40  *Yeshayah* 44:13ff.

But, in the end, one cannot run away from Hashem.

Adam and Chavah tried to run from Hashem, but they found only death and despair outside Gan Eden—only pain and tears.

Our souls come from Heaven, but, being on this earth, there are impediments to understanding. But when we learn Torah, we become a new being, a being on a higher level than we were before. Since we are connected with the Source of life, we rise above what we were one minute ago, above what we thought was possible for us to achieve, above the level of this world—and we enter the world of eternity, infinity.

Torah has done this! Hashem has done this! Only the Jew can attain this level because only the Jew learns Torah and, as we learn, Hashem expands our souls. He gives us this gift called Torah by expanding our mind to encompass what is beyond us, beyond this world.

When we rise to the level that is beyond this world, we are beyond the reach of death. The *yetzer hara* hates this more than anything else, because then we are out of his power! Remember: the *yetzer hara* is also the Angel of Death, the *Malach Ha'maves*. How can he touch us when we are beyond death? We are out of his grasp! He has lost control! Because of this existential threat, the *yetzer hara* must attack Torah. At all costs he must try to separate us from Torah, so that we cannot slip out of his grasp.

My friends, as we said above, the *Aron* in the Beis Hamikdash in Yerushalayim is at the center of the world.

> As the navel is set in the center of the human body, so is the Land of Israel the navel of the world…situated in the center of the world, and Jerusalem in the center of the Land of Israel, and the sanctuary in the center of Yerushalayim, and the holy place in the center of the sanctuary, and the ark in the center of the holy place, and the foundation stone before the holy place, because from it the world was founded.[41]

---

41   *Midrash Tanchuma, Kedoshim.*

> The Sages say: [The world] was created from Tziyon, as it says, "Out of Tziyon, consummation of beauty, from [Tziyon] the beauty of the world was consummated."[42]
>
> Therefore, thus said...Hashem, I have laid a stone for a foundation in Tziyon, a sturdy stone, a precious cornerstone, a secure foundation."[43] This stone is called even shesiyah, which stands at the place of the Aron in the Beis Hamikdash in Yerushalayim. Within the Aron are the two sets of the Luchos received by Moshe at Har Sinai, as it says, "[The second set of] Luchos and the broken pieces of the [first] Luchos [both] rest in the Ark."[44]

Why are the broken *Luchos* in the *Aron*? One might think that the broken *Luchos* have no place in the *Aron*. After all, they were broken! Why do we need reminders in the *Aron* of the terrible moment when B'nei Yisrael rebelled against Hashem? It would seem more appropriate that these reminders of our rebellion should be buried and forgotten rather than being placed in the most prominent spot on the face of the earth!

This is so deep, my friends! This is an eternal lesson to us, to Klal Yisrael, wherever we may be throughout every generation until the end of time. This is what can save us, even when the world seems to be falling apart.

Let's think about what happened with Moshe and those two sets of *Luchos*.

Moshe was on Har Sinai receiving the Torah. Hashem carved two stone *Luchos* and wrote on them. These He gave to Moshe to carry to B'nei Yisrael, and these, along with the teaching Hashem had imparted to Moshe on the mountain, would form the law that would carry B'nei Yisrael on their triumphant march through history as the chosen servants of the Almighty.

---

42  *Yoma* 54b.
43  *Yeshayah* 28:16; see Artscroll commentary on *Yoma* 54b.
44  *Berachos* 8b.

But when Moshe descended from the mountain, he saw that B'nei Yisrael had already strayed from their allegiance to Hashem. Even as Moshe was speaking to Hashem, Moshe's brethren strayed from the very path Hashem was preparing for them.

As the Torah tells us, "It happened as [Moshe] drew near the camp and saw the [Golden] calf and the dances, that Moshe' anger flared up. He threw down the *Luchos* from his hands and shattered them at the foot of the mountain."[45]

Was it then all over?

Of course not. It is never "all over" for us!

Hashem is merciful with His children, even when we make repeated mistakes. And Hashem commanded Moshe to carve a new set of *Luchos*.

> *At that time, Hashem said to me, "Carve for yourself two stone Luchos like the first ones, and ascend to Me to the mountain, and make a wooden Aron for yourself. And I shall inscribe on the Luchos the words that were on the first Luchos that you smashed, and you shall place them in the Aron."*[46]

Let us try to understand what happened here.

The first *Luchos* were about to be given to B'nei Yisrael, and we proved unworthy. Moshe smashed the *Luchos*. It was too much for us to receive the Torah this way. So Hashem told Moshe to carve new *Luchos* and that He would write upon them.

This is the eternal way the Jew learns Torah. This is the paradigm! This is the deepest and most valuable gift we have ever been given! When a Jew learns Torah, it is extremely difficult.

So here is the scenario:

This is what Hashem says to us: "Go learn Torah. I know it seems impossible to grasp it, but try! Even though it is the hardest thing you could ever do, try. Try and try and try and never give up! Try with all

---

45   *Shemos* 32:19.
46   *Devarim* 10:1.

your strength and all your heart. Even if you fail, keep going, for it says,⁴⁷ 'Although the righteous one may fall seven times, he will arise.'"

Hashem says, put every ounce of strength into it, and then, at some point, I am going to give you a gift. I will expand your heart and your mind, and you will begin to understand. Keep doing this your entire life."

The paradigm for this is what happened at Har Sinai when Moshe smashed the *Luchos*.

Moshe had to carve new *Luchos*. Do you think this was easy? Not at all! How did Moshe do it? It was terribly difficult, but Hashem commanded, and he did it. The miracle was that after Moshe carved new *Luchos* with his own hands, Hashem wrote upon them—and they became the basis for the Torah!

This is what we have to do today, every day, when we study Torah. We do this very difficult work of carving out of the stone—our seemingly impenetrable brain, which is blocked by all sorts of spiritual "plaque" and sediment and "spiritual cholesterol." Despite our blocked and stuffed brains, we have to dig and dig and dig and try to understand the Torah, which is the emanation of the Creator of the Universe.

> *If a person sins by having impure thoughts, he causes the radiance...that hovered over his head to depart. However, by totally immersing himself in Torah study, he brings back the holy sparks...which enable him to understand mysteries of the Torah [that he did not understand before]....*⁴⁸

After we carve new *Luchos* out of the "rock" of our closed heart and brain, then we will be rewarded by Hashem, Who will write upon those *Luchos* the words of the Torah. He will open and expand our heart and brain so that we can comprehend the Torah.

As Hashem said to Yehoshua, "This book of the Torah shall not depart from your mouth. Rather, you should contemplate it day and night in

---

47  *Mishlei* 24:16.
48  *Nefesh Hachaim*, gate 1, ch. 20.

order that you observe to do according to all that is written in it, for then you will make your way successful and then you will act wisely."[49]

This is how we can save ourselves in this dark world, in which our hearts and our minds are affected by spiritual pollution, just as the physical environment is being destroyed by physical pollution. Torah is survival. The world cannot live without Torah. Even though we are drowning in moral and spiritual degradation just the way B'nei Yisrael were drowning in impurity in ancient Egypt, still Hashem will rescue us, nationally and individually, just the way He rescued our ancestors in Biblical Egypt.

There is no other hope. Although it may seem impossible, the Torah will rescue us and Hashem will help by opening our hearts and minds so that we can become new people and the world can become a new world of perfect beauty, purity, and peace.

---

[49] *Yehoshua* 1:8.

*Chapter 6*

# SURVIVAL THROUGH ACTS OF KINDNESS

Why do we have such a strong inclination to hate other Jews? We know it is wrong.

Tremendous effort has been expended to eradicate it, but it is not going away.

It is possible that it is stronger than ever.

This inclination is so strong that it caused the destruction of *Bayis Sheini*. The *churban* led to our present exile, which has lasted almost two thousand years, during which occurred the most brutal tortures and tragedies in history.

We have to examine the principle of unity in the world. Unity among B'nei Yisrael is what enabled us to receive the Torah at Har Sinai and to live for centuries in the presence of the Beis Hamikdash. Unity among mankind enables people to live in harmony. "Rabbi Chanina, the deputy Kohel Gadol, says, 'Pray for the welfare of the government, because if people did not fear it, a person would swallow his fellow alive.'"[1]

Democracy has seemed to thrive in the United States. Does the Torah advocate democracy? Does the Torah advocate that we decide policy on the basis of the desire of each individual? I saw that the late Rabbi

---

1   *Pirkei Avos* 3:2.

Avigdor Miller said in one of his *parashah shiurim*, "I am not interested in what you think (or what I think, for that matter). I am interested in what Hashem thinks."

As we say every day, "Hashem annuls the counsel of nations. He balks the designs of peoples. Many designs are in man's heart, but the counsel of Hashem…only it will prevail. The counsel of Hashem will endure forever, the designs of His heart throughout the generations…."[2]

It is only the will of Hashem that rules the world, and the only way we will succeed in this world is if we follow the will of Hashem. That is what Torah is all about.

Most of us have been raised believing that there is wisdom in the vote of the people, but this is not a trustworthy path. The era of democracy is ending as the world slides into chaos.

In Israel, however, the situation is clearer. Israel, as the land given to the Jewish People in the Torah, is by definition the land of Torah, the land in which Torah and the Jewish People are supposed to become one. It is clear that we cannot live successfully there, more than any other place, unless we follow the *ratzon Hashem*, the will of our Creator. We do not make the rules.

Who elected Moshe?

No one! Moshe was singled out by Hashem as the leader of Israel. Hashem said to him, "Now go and I shall dispatch you to Pharaoh and you shall take My people, B'nei Yisrael, out of Egypt."[3]

Who elected Dovid, King of Israel?

Hashem said to Shmuel, "I have seen a king for Myself among [the sons of Yishai]."[4] This is how Dovid was chosen.

This is how our leaders in Eretz Yisrael should be selected, not through an election in which people who hate Hashem appeal to voters and try to shame their opponents. We will have no success if we imitate the foreign cultures who are our enemies. The electoral process stirs up

---

2   *Pesukei D'zimra.*
3   *Shemos* 3:10.
4   *Shmuel I* 16:1.

hatred and bitter rivalry. Why do we do this to each other? Before it is too late, we have to save ourselves from mutual hatred.

I am not advocating suddenly sweeping away the present system; that sudden change would lead to chaos. It is as Hashem says, "I shall not drive…away [the other nations living in Eretz Yisrael] in a single year, lest the land become desolate and the wildlife of the field multiply against you. Little by little shall I drive them away from you, until you become fruitful and make the land your heritage."[5]

But we have to *want* the proper way of life. We have to daven for the proper way of life. We have to realize that the present system is not the Torah system of government and that, in the days of Moshiach, we will not have to endure elections any more, with one Jew fighting another Jew for power and dominance. This is true especially when Torah itself is voted upon! This is a terrible *chillul Hashem*.

Is it a surprise that Moshiach is not here?

These are examples of how the Torah wants us to live:

- "Who is destined for a share in the World to Come? One who is modest and humble, who enters bowing and leaves bowing, who learns Torah constantly but doesn't take credit for himself."[6]
- Before we go to sleep, we say, "Master of the Universe, I hereby forgive anyone who angered or antagonized me or who sinned against me, whether against my body, my property, my honor or against anything of mine, whether he did so accidentally, willfully, carelessly or purposely, whether through speech, deed, thought or notion, whether in this transmigration or another transmigration. I forgive every Jew. May no one be punished because of me."
- The late Rabbi Yisroel Belsky once needed the help of a certain person. A close *talmid* of Rabbi Belsky spent an hour on the phone trying to convince that person to lend his assistance, but he refused. Several weeks later, this same person was dealing with a problem and he sought Rabbi Belsky's help. The *talmid*

---

5   *Shemos* 23:29–30.
6   *Sanhedrin* 88b.

reminded Rabbi Belsky about this man's attitude when he had sought his help. In the *talmid*'s words, "Rabbi Belsky looked at me as if I was out of my mind. 'Are you trying to tell me,' he asked, 'that because he did not help me, I should not help him?'"[7]

Just as it is axiomatic that we as Jews survive through Torah, it is also axiomatic that we survive through *chessed*, meaning mutual kindness and unity. The Talmud tells us that *Bayis Sheini* was destroyed through *sinas chinam*,[8] gratuitous hatred between Jew and Jew. It also tells us that if we have not yet merited to rebuild the Beis Hamikdash, it is because gratuitous hatred persists among us.

We have to know that we are talking about life, death, and eternity. All the horrors of *galus*, up to and including Hitler—may his name be ground to dust—were caused by gratuitous hatred between Jew and Jew.

We received the Torah only because we were united as one nation in brotherhood. At Har Sinai we were *"k'ish echad b'lev echad*—like one man with one heart."[9]

> It is [only] through [the merit of the Jewish People as a whole that] such an attainment [is possible]...that Hashem spoke with [Moshe] only for the sake of the Jewish People.... Thus, all the prestige accorded to Moshe was really in the merit of the Jewish People.[10]

Hashem gave the Torah to the entire nation, not to individuals. Therefore, we must act like one nation in order to reap the benefits of living according to the Torah and in order to avail ourselves of *"Magen Avraham,"* the shield with which Hashem protected Avraham Avinu and with which He protects Avraham's children.[11]

---

7    Rabbi Shimon Finkelman, *Rav Belsky* (NY: Artscroll/Mesorah Publications, 2017), p. 457.
8    *Yoma* 9b.
9    *Rashi* on *Shemos* 19:2.
10   *Ohr Hachaim* on *Vayikra* 1:2.
11   Hashem says to Avraham Avinu in *Bereishis* 15:1, "I am a shield for you." In the merit of our Avos, that shield protects all of Avraham's children, and so the first *berachah* in *Shemoneh Esreh* ends with the words "Shield of Avraham."

The question is this: Since our survival depends on unity, which means caring for each other, why don't we catch on? Why do we act in a way that is harmful to ourselves and prolongs our exile with all its agony?

Let's try to go one step at a time. I want to try to explore the soul of man and discover why the *yetzer hara* is so difficult to dislodge. I want to try to understand how Torah neutralizes the *yetzer hara*. What in fact goes on inside the soul of man that causes our misfortune? Let's try to see how it all works. Let's try to understand *sinas chinam*. Let's try to understand why it is such a challenge for Jews to establish peace and harmony with one another.

I am going to start with myself and give some straightforward examples. Maybe this can be a starting point for our exploration of the human soul.

Sometimes I get angry. I am not happy with myself after I get angry. Is that surprising? Of course not! When the *yetzer hara* grabs us and then we look back at what just happened, we say to ourselves, "I fell down again! I failed!" And that is likely to lead to depression, which is one of the *yetzer hara's* strongest weapons.

As we noted before, every one of us was instructed in the womb by an angel who taught us the entire Torah. When we are born, we forget what the angel taught us and we have to search for it throughout our life. We search for it because we know it is in there somewhere, and we know it is good for us, but we have to find it. We know the truth. We know when we are wrong, and it bothers us.

Let's say that I am driving down the highway and someone is following my car very closely; in other words, "tailgating." He is "pushing" me to go faster. I get angry at this. Yes, tailgating is very dangerous and it is the other guy's fault, but the anger is my fault.

Why am I getting angry? Just because he did something wrong doesn't mean that I need to get angry. Why do I hate the person who is following my car? Why do my emotions get involved?

This question, I believe, is very important. We have to separate the objective facts of this case from emotion. It is one thing that this person did something bad, but it is another thing to hate him.

Here's another example. I am davening up by the front wall of the shul. The *tefillah* has finished and most people have left the room. There are reading lights over the desk where the *baal tefillah* had been standing. Someone wants to turn them off after the *tefillah*, but I am still davening right next to those lights. Instead of going around behind me to reach the switch, he reaches in front of my face, which disturbs my prayer.

I become angry. He should have walked behind me. I think, "He is such a bad person," and I have negative thoughts about him.

Why am I angry?

Above, I quoted *K'rias Shema al Hamitah*, the *tefillah* we say at bedtime, which has an amazing passage. This is what we are supposed to have in mind as we are falling asleep: "Master of the Universe, I hereby forgive anyone who angered or antagonized me or who sinned against me…I forgive every Jew. May no man be punished because of me…."

At night, when we sleep, our souls return to *Shamayim*. We prepare for that journey by trying to erase all animosity toward our fellow Jew. We cannot enter Hashem's Presence while we harbor ill-will toward our brother or sister…even if the other person is at fault!

"[Anger] is a terrible trait, and a person must distance himself until the extreme and teach himself not to become angry even when called for."[12]

The Torah wants us to separate ourselves from anger and hatred.

Not only that, but before we begin to daven, we are supposed to do the same thing. We are supposed to erase all animosity toward our brethren before we speak to the King of kings. Rabbi Chaim Vital says, "Before a person arranges his prayer in shul…one must accept…to love your neighbor as yourself and be prepared to love every member of Klal Yisrael."[13]

We have already mentioned above that while the Jews stood before Hashem at Har Sinai, there was perfect harmony among them.

---

12  Rambam, *Hilchos Deos* 2:4.
13  Rabbi Chaim Vital, *Sha'ar Hakavanos*.

Clearly, it is not easy to eradicate the feelings of hatred and anger that lead to separation. Otherwise the Torah would not need to point out specifically how vital it is to do so.

So where does this feeling come from? What is the story of this deep and dark reservoir of anger that seems to reside within us, the reservoir from which we draw the poison called *sinas chinam*?

The amazing thing is that all the things I hate in others, I do myself!

On the basis of that, I would like to tell you my theory.

Let's start with the tailgating driver.

Let's say that I am driving. What happens if there is someone driving very slowly in front of me? It happened yesterday, and I can tell you that I was angry. "Why is he driving so slowly? What gives him the right to hold up the entire street?" My reaction is to pressure him to drive faster or move over. In other words, I got angry at the tailgater described above, but here I became the tailgater myself! I am tailgating another guy because I think he is driving too slowly! I am doing the same thing that I got angry about!

In other words, I get angry at others because I see in them the terrible trait that I know is in me! I don't want to face it in myself, so I "put it" on others and blame them!

Let's take the second example, the one who turned off the light. Do you think I am so careful about getting in front of someone else when *he* is davening? Do you think I am so careful about other people's feelings and sensitivities?

I remember one occasion when I came into the shul upset. I remembered that I had left some books and reading glasses somewhere in the shul. I grabbed them from where they were sitting, but, in my rush, I dropped them on the floor. This was directly in front of someone else who was in the middle of *Shemoneh Esreh*. Afterward, he was upset with me, and he had good reason to be upset. I had reached in front of him when he was praying and, in addition, had dropped my belongings on the ground and disrupted his *tefillah*.

The same thing that had angered me, I myself had done to someone else. My anger mirrored my own trait. I had done the same thing to someone else, and then I was angry at him for doing what I myself had done.

I get angry at others for my own bad traits that I see in them. I am seeing my own faults in others, and that is what makes me angry! I don't want to face my own faults, so rather than working on myself to get rid of them, I get angry at others for having those very same faults.

This is a direct cause of *sinas chinam*.

This is an important idea that I would like to explore further. The first thing to investigate is whether there is a basis for this idea in the Torah.

The first brotherly hatred in the Torah is between Kayin and Hevel. Hevel brought a sacrifice to Hashem "from the very best…of the flock," but Kayin's offering was relatively worthless, "without troubling to choose the finest."[14] When Kayin was punished by Hashem for murdering his brother, he was "annoyed" at Hashem for punishing him.[15] Why was he annoyed? "Through jealousy of his brother's acceptability."[16] But who caused Kayin to give an inferior offering? "Why do you indulge in self-pity? The option is yours to rise above your brother,"[17] said Hashem, "but you did not take that option."

People become angry at others because of their own faults.

The classic case of brotherly hatred, which stands at the beginning of Jewish history and influences our fate to this very day, is the story of Yosef and his brothers. Why did Yosef employ a roundabout method of bringing his brothers to repentance? Why did they immediately respond by admitting to themselves their own guilt? Did that follow from Yosef's accusations?

Let's begin with the brothers' original complaint against Yosef. Was Yaakov at fault for giving Yosef "a fine woolen tunic?" Was he wrong to love "Yosef more than all of his sons, since he was a child of his old age?"[18] The *Ramban* says that "this is the reason for the hatred of the brothers toward [their] younger brother."[19]

---

14   Rabbi Samson Raphael Hirsch on *Bereishis* 4:3.
15   *Bereishis* 4:5.
16   *Seforno*.
17   *Abarbanel*.
18   *Bereishis* 37:3.
19   *Ramban* on *Bereishis* 37:3.

In truth, Yosef's brothers had some reason for resenting him. For one thing, they were jealous of the special status their father had given him. Second, they resented his dreams, in which his father, mother, and brothers bowed down to him, which implied an attitude of domination over them. In addition, he brought "evil reports"[20] about them to his father.

So there seems to have been cause for the brothers to think evil about Yosef and to be angry at him. But the problem became worse, and the brothers actually considered killing Yosef. Finally, they sold him. He went into slavery in Egypt and they eventually followed him. This was the first exile of B'nei Yisrael.

At this point, let's make the distinction between a legitimate grievance and *sinas chinam*, unwarranted hatred. The reason that we went into exile and are suffering from terrible tragedy, the reason the Beis Hamikdash was destroyed, is *sinas chinam*, unwarranted hatred between Jew and Jew.

Warranted hatred is different, and there are ways to resolve legitimate grievances, including face-to-face discussion. As the *Ramban* says, ordinarily the brothers would have "argued with" Yosef and "rebuked him, and he would have had to stop, and their resentment would have been removed. However [in this case, things could not be resolved in this way] because of the added factor that [Yaakov] loved [Yosef] more than all his brothers.... This is what the verse means when it says, 'And they could not speak to him,'" which is the normal way of making peace.

Let's see what happens next. These are the dynamics of *sinas chinam*, gratuitous hatred. There may have been a provocation. This is already a problem. But, once provoked, let us see how the problem mushrooms.

Let's keep in mind the fact that hatred among the brothers is what propelled us into our original exile in Egypt. This is the prototype of all the exiles that will ever be. It was generated by hatred among the brothers. This is a lesson of the most profound gravity. The Torah is telling us that our problems today are based on this episode in the Torah.

---

20  *Bereishis* 37:2.

If that is so, we can learn how to save ourselves on this very day, today, by studying this episode. We have to go into it and learn about it and apply it to ourselves. With Hashem's help, we will finally save ourselves, now at the end of history, when the challenges are greater than ever, when the entire world is turning against us, and all our lives are at stake.

After hearing Yosef's dream, the brothers said, "Would you reign over us? Would you…dominate us?" And the Torah adds, "And they hated him even more." This apparently means that they hated him because of their father's special love for him, but now, in addition, they hated him because they felt that he wanted to rule over them. This already crosses over into the area of "*sinas chinam*—groundless hatred." Notice that the Torah writes "hated" exactly after "Would you reign over us?" This indicates the hatred was related to their perception that Yosef wanted to reign over them.

Did Yosef do anything bad to his brothers?

Not only did he not do anything bad to his brothers, but his desire was to do good for them. In fact, later, when he became viceroy in Egypt, he saved them. His alleged "domination" was to be for their good in every way.

The brothers saw in his dreams that he was destined for greatness and they wanted to pull him down. According to the *Ohr Hachaim*, "With this [second] dream, they let go of the thoughts [that Yosef wanted to rule over them], for [Yosef] certainly did not think…to lord it over his father. So [they realized that] this [dream] could only be a message from Heaven, and they therefore grew jealous [of Yosef]." As the Torah specifically says, "His brothers were jealous of him."[21]

This is what we call *sinas chinam,* gratuitous hatred. There was no reason for it. It was not based on an evil deed, or even thought, on the part of Yosef. It was based only on the brothers' perception of his personal qualities of greatness, and it was based on the prophetic nature of his dreams, which indicated future greatness and, indeed, domination.

---

21   *Bereishis* 37:11.

The challenge in our life is not to envy someone else's success. To be *samei'ach b'chelko*, happy with one's lot in life, is not only the key to peace of mind, but it is the key to ending *sinas chinom*, gratuitous hatred, among us.

When Yosef told his brothers about his dreams, this did not emanate from a desire to dominate them. "Perhaps Yosef meant to inform them that it was [a decree] of Heaven that he was [to be] raised up [to greatness], and Yaakov's action [of overly favoring Yosef over his brothers] was with the consent of the Upper Realms, and [Yosef thought that] as a result of [hearing] this, [his brothers] would stop hating him."[22]

However, as a result of their jealousy, the brothers came close to killing Yosef and then sent him to Egypt as a slave. When they met him next, he was viceroy of Egypt, and all their fears concerning his domination were in fact fulfilled. But this domination was, in the end, their salvation.

His method of sending a healing message to them was to subdue them and make them all feel powerless, which corresponded with what they had accused him of desiring to do to them.

We should note the amazing parallel between the brothers' accusation against Yosef and the words of the *nachash* in Gan Eden. The snake was basically saying that Hashem desired to dominate Adam and Chavah. In the words of Rabbi Samson Raphael Hirsch, the snake was saying, "Hashem did not prohibit this tree out of any concern for your lives, but because He is aware that by eating from it you will attain extra wisdom and become omniscient like Him. Then you will be independent of Him."[23]

Let me share a personal story. I had the opportunity to visit the White House when my father received the National Medal of the Arts from President George W. Bush in 2007. I had a personal conversation with the president at a time when he was receiving heavy criticism from the media. I told him why, in my opinion, he was receiving so much criticism. I said it was because he believes in G-d and holds moral principles

---

22   *Ohr Hachaim* on *Bereishis* 37:5.
23   Rabbi Samson Raphael Hirsch on *Bereishis* 3:4.

based on the Bible. His critics did not share his beliefs and were trying to pull him down to their level. In this way, I tried to encourage him.[24]

This is a similar phenomenon to the confrontation between Yosef and his brothers. They could not tolerate the idea of his dominance over them, even if he had no selfish or evil intent, even if he had no personal desire for power, even if he did not hurt them, even if—to the contrary—his actions saved them, their families, and their descendants.

This is *sinas chinam*, the inevitable results of which are slavery and exile, and we see the textbook case here with Yosef and his brothers. The direct result of trying to pull someone else down is that you become a slave and are yourself dominated by the one whom you accused of wanting to dominate you. This occurred in Gan Eden and this occurred with Yosef and his brothers.

> *The psychological insights of our Torah scholars are amazing.... It should therefore not amaze us to find that people well-versed in Torah had a profound understanding of human nature and behavior.... The Baal Shem Tov taught that the world is a mirror, and that the defects we see in other people are only a reflection of our own defects. We are likely to be oblivious to our own defects, but can easily detect shortcomings in other people. The Baal Shem Tov instructs us to take such observations as indications that we have these shortcomings ourselves.*[25]

In other words, if you desire to do *teshuvah*, then observe your criticism of others and you will see your own faults.

The following Gemara seems to support this same insight:

> *Whoever declares others [to be genealogically] unfit is [himself genealogically] unfit.... And Shmuel said: He declares [them] unfit with his own blemish.... [Rav Nachman asked*

---

24  One of his staff members later told me that my words were greatly appreciated by the president.
25  Rabbi Abraham J. Twerski, MD, from an article in *Jewish Action*, Spring 1966.

> Rav Yehudah:] Why did master proclaim that [a certain person] was a slave? [Rav Yehudah] answered him: Because he frequently calls people slaves, and a Tanna has taught in a Beraisa: Anyone who declares [others to be genealogically] unfit is [himself] unfit....And Shmuel said: With his own blemish he declares [others] unfit.[26]

What does this insight mean? How can we understand this? How can it help us?

Once we see that the qualities that we hate in others are qualities that we hate in ourselves, we can start to work on ourselves to rid ourselves of these traits.

Here is our general principle: When we hate someone, we are hating that same trait in ourselves.

It is fascinating that there is a commandment to "hate Amalek."[27] This is one of the 613 mitzvos. This commandment indicates we do not naturally hate others. We have to be commanded by Hashem to hate Amalek, but in the ordinary makeup of the Jew, there is no natural place for hatred.

Hatred is out of place in us and is an aberration.

The same process also goes for other emotions, like fear. In other words, when we fear others, we are actually fearing the *yetzer hara* within ourselves. In other words, we are fearing ourselves.

When I was young, I used to be afraid of getting beaten up by street kids, what we then called "juvenile delinquents." I was afraid that I would be beaten up by evil people. It never happened, but I replayed over and over in my mind the scenario of being threatened and how I would respond. In the scenario, I was always speaking with them and trying to convince them how illogical it was to beat me up.

I know that I was afraid of myself. I was afraid that inside I was actually violent, that there was a "being" in there which I could not control, the "real me" who was dangerous and could not be controlled and would

---

26  *Kiddushin* 70a/b.
27  *Devarim* 25:18.

lash out violently at others. I was afraid that I myself was this evil and dangerous being and that I was out of control. I was afraid of myself.

You could say this was not logical, because it wasn't so crazy to be afraid of being beaten up. People did get beaten up. But my fear was more than what was warranted by the facts. There can be such a thing as fear that is independent of the facts. I remind you, my readers, of the famous remark, uttered by US President Franklin D. Roosevelt, "The only thing we have to fear is fear itself."[28] Fear can have a life of its own apart from the reality of that which is the object of fear. And fear can paralyze.

If fear were insignificant, then why would Dovid HaMelech have said, "Hashem is with me; I have no fear. How can man affect me?"[29] Fear of man is in conflict with *yiras Shamayim*, fear of Heaven. Fear of man is in conflict with the service of Hashem.

We can trace fear to the same place within us that we can trace hatred of others, the *yetzer hara*. Isn't this logical? The *yetzer hara* is the source of instability and trouble. It is by definition out of our control, so the condition of man in this world is that we are afraid of the *yetzer hara*, which means that we are afraid of ourselves.

Why is fear of the *yetzer hara* equivalent to fear of ourselves? The method of operation of the *yetzer hara* is that we come to believe that the "real me" is the *yetzer hara*, that my nature is intrinsically evil and therefore there is no hope for me. This leads to despair and paralysis, G-d forbid.

In Gan Eden, the *yetzer hara* was an independent entity, a separate creature. Since Gan Eden was perfect, there was nothing intrinsically evil there. But Hashem created us with free will, and thus the capacity to choose to obey or not to obey Him. When Chavah and then Adam chose to rebel, the *yetzer hara* entered into them and became a source of evil—in fact they ingested the forbidden fruit—and when they were expelled from Gan Eden, they carried the fruit of their rebellion within

---

28  During his 1933 inaugural address.
29  *Tehillim* 118.

them. Thus, the *yetzer hara* became part of mankind after our expulsion from Gan Eden, and the source of our trouble is within ourselves.

There is, however, a way to approach this.

Please contemplate this remarkable letter the Chazon Ish wrote to one of his students:

> *Strengthen yourself, my dear one, strengthen yourself, and envelop yourself with the fortitude to engross yourself in Torah, for it is for that purpose you were created. With just a little more [effort] you will be able to come to grips with your evil inclination. Then his defeat will be total, and he will no longer bother you. Just overcome him today and he will be your faithful servant for all time.*[30]

Let's explore how bringing Torah inside us enables us to overcome the *yetzer hara*. We say every day in our prayers, "Let not the evil inclination dominate us. Distance us from an evil person and an evil companion. Attach us to the good inclination and to good deeds, and compel our evil inclination to be subservient to You." This means it is possible not only to overcome the *yetzer hara*, but, in the words of the Chazon Ish, to make it "our servant," and direct that vast power toward life instead of death.

> *The Holy One, blessed be He, said to Israel, "My son, I have created the evil inclination and I have created Torah 'tavlin,' as its antidote. If you involve yourselves in Torah, you will not be delivered into its hand…but if you do not involve yourselves in Torah, you will be delivered into its hand."*[31]

It is a lifelong effort to involve oneself in Torah to a greater and greater degree, but clearly it is attainable, because Hashem Himself says it is attainable, and we know that *tzaddikim* have attained mastery over their *yetzer hara*. As we say every day, "Blessed are You, Hashem…Who has…commanded us to engross ourselves in the words of Torah."[32]

---

30 Rabbi Shlomo Lorincz, *In Their Shadow* (Jerusalem: Feldheim Publishers, 2008), p. 33.
31 *Kiddushin* 30b.
32 *Shacharis*.

Let's understand why the Gemara calls Torah "*tavlin*," which means spice or condiment. How does this make sense, and how can it help us achieve our goal of mastery over our *yetzer hara*? If Torah is a weapon with which we can defeat and subdue the *yetzer hara*, then why doesn't the Gemara call it that? Is it minimizing the role of Torah to refer to it as *tavlin,* a condiment?

I would like to suggest the following: Hashem, the One who created the *yetzer hara*, is the Power who controls it. But how do we reach Hashem? He is beyond us, totally. Even Moshe Rabbeinu could approach Hashem only indirectly. No man can be in His Presence, because then we would cease to exist. But our goal is to be close to Him. To be close to Him is our life's work. As Dovid HaMelech says, "*Achas shoalti*—One thing I asked of Hashem, that shall I seek: that I dwell in the House of Hashem all the days of my life, to behold the sweetness of Hashem and to contemplate in His Sanctuary."[33]

Although we can seek to "dwell in His house," we cannot stand in front of Him. It is beyond us. But one thing we can do—we can become part of Torah. We can make it part of us and become part of it. As we say in the *Hadran*,[34] "We shall return to you and you shall return to us. Our thoughts are on you and your thoughts are on us. We will not forget you and you will not forget us, neither in this world nor in the World to Come." We are speaking to the Gemara like our most trusted friend.

Indeed, it is!

We want to become one with Hashem, so He sends His trusted servant, the Torah, to us, and the Torah makes Hashem "accessible" to us, so to speak.

Please listen to the words of Rabbi Avigdor Miller:

> *How can anybody know what Hashem is thinking?...But He wants us to think what He is thinking. That is what He wrote in the Torah! Our career in this world is to adopt the attitudes of Hakadosh Baruch Hu as our own. And Hashem was now*

---

33 *Tehillim* 27.
34 The *Hadran* is recited when one concludes a tractate in the Gemara.

*going to provide us a model: "Anochi. I am the only model. Follow Me!".... Hashem's perfect thoughts are infinite, and therefore we have to get busy thinking along with the Torah. To mold our minds into Torah minds, minds that work according to the guidelines of Hashem's thoughts is a lifetime of work....*[35]

Torah is the "condiment," the spice[36] that makes it possible to swallow "the thoughts of Hashem" and make them part of us.

We can learn from the order of putting on tefillin the process by which we absorb Torah attitudes and thoughts:

- First, the tefillin are placed on the arm next to the heart, the seat of emotion.
- Second, the tefillin are placed on the head, next to the brain, the seat of thought and intellect.
- Third, the straps are wrapped around the arm and hand, which represent action.

What does this mean?

There are three paragraphs in the *Shema*.

The first paragraph begins, "And you shall love Hashem, your G-d, with all your heart, with all your soul and with all your resources."[37] Everything begins with love. Our goal in life is to love Hashem. If we love evil things, G-d forbid, it is all over; we will be brought into the pit of destruction and our life will be evil and cause evil. That is why we say every day that we want to train ourselves to love Hashem and to go after His ways. That is what we signify when we place the tefillin on our arm next to our heart. That is how we want our life to be. As we say in the third paragraph, "Do not follow after your heart and after your eyes after which you stray."[38]

---

35  Rabbi Avigdor Miller on *Parashas Ki Sisa*.
36  Many ancient (and even modern) remedies are made from spices.
37  *Devarim* 6:5.
38  *Bamidbar* 15:39.

If our heart and our eyes lead us, then we will be attached to the material things we see in this world and we will be lost. But if we train our heart to go after Torah, we will be saved. Since the seat of love is the heart, the tefillin are placed first near the heart and the first paragraph of the *Shema* deals with the emotions of the heart, which must be directed to Hashem.

The second paragraph deals with "hearkening to My commandments." That is Torah, and that corresponds to the second step of tefillin, which is placing it upon the head, the seat of the brain, where we learn Torah. If we devote our heart to loving Hashem and our brain to encompassing the Torah, then we are on the path of healing and a meaningful existence. All will be well if we hearken to Hashem's commandments.

The third step in tefillin is to bind the straps to our hand, which corresponds to carrying out the commandments through all our actions. This corresponds to the third paragraph of the *Shema*, which emphasizes that we are obligated to "remember all the commandments of Hashem and perform them...."[39]

By wearing tefillin and accepting upon ourselves the obligation to incorporate within ourselves the "thoughts of Hashem," we are attempting to purify ourselves and eliminate the influence of the *yetzer hara*. If we are willing to give up our own thoughts, our "baby thoughts" (in the words of Rabbi Avigdor Miller), and we try to rise toward the level of the Supreme Intelligence and think His thoughts, then we are going to subdue the influence of the *yetzer hara* and eliminate the causes of gratuitous hatred that divides us.

To sum up: If you are angry at someone, it is likely that you are angry at yourself. If you hate someone, it is likely that you hate their qualities that you see in yourself. If you are afraid of someone, it is likely that you are afraid of yourself.

However, the more we connect to Hashem and we think His thoughts, then the anger turns to calmness, the hate turns to love, and the fear

---

39   *Bamidbar* 15:40.

of people turns to fear of Hashem. With this inside us, we can become one again, because the source of hatred and division has been erased.

Knowing this is the key to healing our division as a nation and bringing Moshiach.

"Praise Hashem, all nations. Praise Him, all the states. For His kindness has overwhelmed us and the truth of Hashem is eternal."[40] How does Hashem's kindness "overwhelm" us? Our mind is filled with Torah and all evil is eliminated by the Shechinah just the way darkness is eliminated by the presence of light.

Let's conclude this chapter with one additional thought. We have discussed *Rashi*'s comment concerning the unity of B'nei Yisrael at Har Sinai. We were then "like one man with one heart,"[41] and through our unity we merited that Hashem gave His "fiery Torah" to us.[42]

What does it mean that we were "like one man with one heart?"

Every person can understand this. No person hates his own body. As we saw with the tefillin, all the parts of our body can work together, not only for physical health, but for the performance of mitzvos and for spiritual welfare, our closeness to Hashem. No part of the body is jealous of another part. Our foot is not jealous of our hand, nor is our mouth jealous of our eye.

Each has its function; together they operate as one organic unit.

The Torah wants us to understand that this concept applies to all of Klal Yisrael together. We are like an individual body, "one man with one heart." If we function as an organic whole, with no jealousy among the parts and each individual organ performing its unique and necessary function, then we will be healthy spiritually and physically.

That is what Hashem wants and that is what we need. We need to be that organic unit in order to survive and merit to return to our Holy Land in peace and assume our rightful place as the emissaries of Hashem and the spiritual leaders of the world.

---

40   *Tehillim* 117.
41   *Rashi* on *Shemos* 19:2.
42   *Devarim* 33:2.

*Chapter 7*

# SHEMONEH ESREH AS A LIFE PRESERVER

Let us review the daily *Shemoneh Esreh*, the main part of every prayer service, and understand how each of the nineteen *berachos* can play a part in our survival in this dangerous world.

This *tefillah*, which originated with our Avos, Avraham, Yitzchak and Yaakov, was subsequently transformed into its present *nusach* by the Anshei Knesses Hagedolah. As it says:

> *Shimon Hapakuli arranged the eighteen blessings in order before Rabban Gamliel in Yavneh. Rabbi Yochanan said, and some say that it was taught in a Beraisa: One hundred and twenty elders, among whom were many prophets, formulated eighteen blessings in a [specific] order.*[1]

Our Avos and great *rabbonim* foresaw, through *nevuah, ruach hakodesh* and exalted insight, the long years during which B'nei Yisrael would suffer terribly in *galus*. They therefore sustained us with this lifesaving *tefillah*.

"One should not rise to pray other than with an attitude of reverence. The early pious ones would tarry for one hour and [then] pray, in order

---

1   *Megillah* 17b.

that they might direct their hearts to their Father in Heaven."[2] We would do well to try to arrange our emotions before we address our Creator, so that we approach Him with the understanding that all our success in life depends upon our relationship with Him. *"Ein od milvado*—Hashem, He is G-d; there is none beside Him."[3]

## THE FIRST BERACHAH: THE AVOS

This *berachah* speaks about the Avos, but the real subject is Hashem.

In a world of darkness, the Avos discovered Hashem, and thus we begin these prayers with the words:

בָּרוּךְ אַתָּה ה' אֱ-לֹהֵינוּ וֵא-לֹהֵי אֲבוֹתֵינוּ, אֱ-לֹהֵי אַבְרָהָם, אֱ-לֹהֵי יִצְחָק, וֵא-לֹהֵי יַעֲקֹב, הָאֵ-ל הַגָּדוֹל הַגִּבּוֹר וְהַנּוֹרָא, אֵ-ל עֶלְיוֹן, גּוֹמֵל חֲסָדִים טוֹבִים, וְקוֹנֵה הַכֹּל, וְזוֹכֵר חַסְדֵי אָבוֹת, וּמֵבִיא גוֹאֵל לִבְנֵי בְנֵיהֶם לְמַעַן שְׁמוֹ בְּאַהֲבָה:

מֶלֶךְ עוֹזֵר וּמוֹשִׁיעַ וּמָגֵן: בָּרוּךְ אַתָּה ה' מָגֵן אַבְרָהָם.

*Blessed are You, Hashem our G-d and the G-d of our fathers, G-d of Avraham, G-d of Yitzchak, and G-d of Yaakov; the great, the mighty and awesome G-d; the supreme G-d, Who bestows benevolent kindness and controls everything; Who recalls the devotion of the Patriarchs and brings a redeemer to their children's children for the sake of His Name, with love.*

*O King, Helper, Savior, and Protector. Blessed are You, Hashem, Shield of Avraham.*

The first thing to know is that there is a Creator who guides the world with total control. If we know that, then we know where to seek help, and that address is available to us at all times and in all places. If Hashem created us, then He obviously wants us to live, and if He has total control, then He is able to help without limitation. Also, He "bestows

---

2   *Berachos* 30b.
3   *Devarim* 4:35.

beneficial kindnesses," a trait He taught to the Avos, and therefore He wants to help.

When we say this *berachah*, we should have in mind the fundamental thought that there is an all-powerful Source of help for us. We should keep in mind that the Avos, especially Avraham, were alone in a world that ridiculed the idea of monotheism to such an extent that it had completely abandoned Hashem's laws and therefore worshipped idols.

Today also, almost the entire world ridicules us, the Jews. But Hashem protects those who love and obey Him, just as He protected the Avos, and that is why the *berachah* ends with the words, "*Magen Avraham*—Shield of Avraham." Just as Hashem was the Shield of Avraham against all who hated him, so will He be our Shield, if we obey His laws.

That is our basic source of strength and consolation.

This *berachah* states that Hashem will send a redeemer to the "children's children" of the Avos. We are those "children's children." This is a great source of comfort. It reinforces at the beginning of the *Shemoneh Esreh* that Hashem will bring the redeemer.

But there is more.

Please note the language: Hashem will bring a redeemer to the Avos's children's children *"lema'an Shemo b'ahavah*—for the sake of His Name, with love." That is a huge statement. That means that even if we do not deserve the redeemer, Hashem is going to send him!

What does "for His Name's sake" mean? It means that *galus* is a diminution of Hashem's Name, that His children, to whom He gave six hundred thirteen mitzvos, rebelled against Him! As a result, He took our Beis Hamikdash away from us and exiled us from our land.

It is, to be sure, an embarrassment, *kavyochol*, for our Father in Heaven that we rejected His Torah enough to warrant this terrible punishment, so at some point He is going to "rescue His Name" and bring us back to our land, because Hashem's Name must be restored to its status.

This resembles the situation in Egypt, where—although we had sunk to the forty-ninth level of impurity—Hashem still rescued us in the merit of our ancestors, the Avos with whom He had made a *bris*.

> For although the time that He had decreed for them [to be in exile in Egypt] had been completed, they were [nevertheless] not fit to be redeemed [at that point], as is stated explicitly by [the Prophet] Yechezkel,[4] but, because of [our] outcry [to Him], He accepted [our] prayers, in His mercy.[5]

The promise to redeem us, even though we may not deserve it, is a huge source of comfort.

The first *berachah* of *Shemoneh Esreh* ends with four amazing words: מלך עוזר ומושיע ומגן, followed by: ברוך אתה ה' מגן אברהם.

"מלך—King": If we accept Hashem as our King, all the deficiencies in our life will be remedied, and He will lead us to spiritual and physical safety and security. It is an overriding source of strength to know that we have a completely benevolent and powerful King.

"עוזר—Helper": We can turn to Him for help at all times. He is always available.

"ומושיע—Savior": Hashem is going to save us. We must keep asking Him to save us. We have to know that in all situations, He is to be called upon. Sometimes one can feel spiritually powerless. But Hashem is perpetually powerful and therefore, regardless of how ineffectual we may feel at any moment, we should remain aware that He is always able to save us.

"ומגן—Shield [of Avraham]": In a world full of hatred and danger, He is our shield. He protected Avraham Avinu when he was alone in a world of idolaters who wanted to kill him, and so, if we turn to Him, He will protect us, against all odds. As Dovid HaMelech tells us, "Some [depend on] chariots and some [depend on] horses, but we call out in the Name of Hashem."[6]

---

4　Yechezkel 20:8.
5　Ramban on *Shemos* 2:25.
6　Tehillim 20.

## THE SECOND BERACHAH: STRENGTH AND ETERNAL LIFE

אַתָּה גִּבּוֹר לְעוֹלָם אֲ-דֹנָי, מְחַיֶּה מֵתִים אַתָּה, רַב לְהוֹשִׁיעַ, מְכַלְכֵּל חַיִּים בְּחֶסֶד, מְחַיֶּה מֵתִים בְּרַחֲמִים רַבִּים, סוֹמֵךְ נוֹפְלִים, וְרוֹפֵא חוֹלִים, וּמַתִּיר אֲסוּרִים, וּמְקַיֵּם אֱמוּנָתוֹ לִישֵׁנֵי עָפָר, מִי כָמוֹךָ בַּעַל גְּבוּרוֹת וּמִי דּוֹמֶה לָּךְ, מֶלֶךְ מֵמִית וּמְחַיֶּה וּמַצְמִיחַ יְשׁוּעָה: וְנֶאֱמָן אַתָּה לְהַחֲיוֹת מֵתִים: בָּרוּךְ אַתָּה ה', מְחַיֶּה הַמֵּתִים:

*You are mighty forever, O G-d; You revive the dead, and are abundantly able to save. Who sustains life with kindness, revives the deceased with abundant mercy, supports the fallen, heals the sick, releases the bound, and maintains His faith with those asleep in the dust. Who is like You, Master of mighty deeds! Who can be compared to You, King Who causes death and life, and causes salvation to sprout! And You are faithful to revive the dead. Blessed are You, Hashem, Who revives the dead.*

If Hashem created the entire universe out of nothing, then we can understand that He certainly has the strength to bring back to life those who have died. This means that the end of life…is not the end.

This has to be real to us, because it is crucial to maintaining feelings of hope and purity of action under all conditions. If death is the end of life, then we lose hope. There is no point in living if everything ends at the grave. We may as well spend our entire life in pursuit of physical pleasures if our body is all that exists.

There is more. If the world looks hopeless, which it does now and has before, we should know that there is hope beyond hope. How did we go on after the destruction of the First and Second Beis Hamikdash? There was apparently no hope! We went on because Hashem's strength is beyond this world and everything in it.

There is an amazing story about Rabbi Yosef Yitzchak Schneersohn,[7] who heard banging on his front door one night. A squad of Russian

---

7   The sixth rebbe of Lubavitch (1880–1950).

secret police entered, placing him under arrest for the "crime" of learning and spreading Torah. One of his interrogators put a gun to his head and said, "this toy has a way of making people cooperate." The rebbe answered calmly: "That toy is persuasive to one who has many gods and only one world. I have One G-d and two worlds."[8]

The power of these words is incredible because the person who spoke them knew that he was beyond the reach of any man. Anyone who cleaves to Hashem is protected eternally, under all circumstances.

The point is that we have to know that we are protected. It is not easy to achieve this power of mind and understanding; it represents a lifetime of work, but it is our legacy and the basis of our hope.

When Moshiach comes, the righteous will arise from their graves:

> *The hand of Hashem was upon me. It took me out by the spirit of Hashem and set me in the midst of a valley, and it was filled with bones. He passed me over them all around and around, and behold, they were very numerous...and, behold, they were very dry. Then He said to me: "Son of Man, can these bones come to life?" And I said: "Lord, Hashem: You know!"*
>
> *He said to me: "Prophesy over these bones. Say to them, 'O dry bones, hear the word of Hashem. Behold...you will come to life...." So I prophesied as I was commanded.... There was a sound...then, behold, there was a noise and the bones drew near, each bone to its [matching] bone. Then...skin...covered them...but there was no spirit in them.... Then He said to me: "Prophesy to the spirit...." I prophesied...and the spirit entered them and they came to life. They stood upon their feet, a very, very great legion.*
>
> *He said to me: "Son of Man, these bones, they are the whole House of Israel.... Then you will know that I am Hashem, when I open your graves and when I raise you up from your*

---

8   Heard from Rabbi Ephraim Wachsman.

graves, My People...then you will know that I Hashem have spoken and I have fulfilled...."[9]

As we say at the very end of the Pesach Seder in the song *Chad Gadya*, Hashem will slay death itself. In order for us to survive against all odds, when the entire world is against us, we have to know that, whatever happens, Hashem will bring those back to life who were true to Him and His Torah.

During the winter months, we insert in this *berachah* the words "*Mashiv haruach u'morid ha'geshem*—[Hashem] causes the wind to blow and the rain to fall."

Why are storm and rain mentioned at this point?

Storm and rain are direct conduits of the blessing that enables all life on earth. Rain is compared to Torah; it gives life. "May My teaching drop like the rain; may My utterance flow like the dew."[10] Rain is compared to the resurrection of the dead because it brings life to the dead earth.

The weather forecaster on the radio talks like this: "This weekend will be a washout. No beach days! The miserable weather will continue until...." But those who live in the Land of Israel, *lehavdil*, know that rain is a blessing from Heaven.[11]

Our rabbis teach us, "There are three keys in the hand of the Holy One, blessed be He, that are not entrusted to an agent. They are the key of rain, the key of childbirth, and the key of revival of the dead."[12] Rain is on a level with childbirth and the revival of the dead. The key to life can be found in the *Shemoneh Esreh*. Our rabbis show us what to ask for.

## THE THIRD BERACHAH: THE HOLINESS OF HASHEM'S NAME

אַתָּה קָדוֹשׁ, וְשִׁמְךָ קָדוֹשׁ, וּקְדוֹשִׁים בְּכָל יוֹם יְהַלְלוּךָ סֶּלָה: בָּרוּךְ אַתָּה ה' הָאֵ-ל הַקָּדוֹשׁ:

---

9   *Yechezkel* 37:1ff.
10  *Devarim* 32:2.
11  No matter where one lives, rain in the proper measure is a blessing, but in the Land of Israel, rain is apparently particularly dependent upon the spiritual condition of the Jews.
12  *Taanis* 2a.

> *You are holy, and Your Name is holy, and holy ones praise You every day, forever. Blessed are You, Hashem, the Almighty Who is holy.*

What does this mean? I believe this is a very deep concept. The commentary in the Artscroll siddur says, "The 'Name of Hashem' refers to the manner in which we perceive His actions."

Hashem "appears" in various ways to the people who dwell on this earth. Avraham Avinu found out through his own mental and spiritual processes that Hashem must exist.

Hashem spoke to Avraham, Yitzchak, and Yaakov. Hashem spoke to Moshe. Hashem spoke to every prophet. Hashem appeared to Moshe in the burning bush. Hashem rescued His children from Egypt and they all saw him at Yam Suf, as it says, "Israel saw the great hand that Hashem inflicted upon Egypt...."[13] And then Hashem appeared at Har Sinai "in the thickness of the cloud."[14] We daven every day that the Shechinah should return to Har Habayis.

All these things appear to be impossible. Hashem is invisible and not material. How can He "appear"?

This, I believe, is what is meant by "the Holiness of Hashem's Name." There is some way that the Shechinah becomes manifest in this world. When you go through the normal experiences of life, you are not always aware of the Shechinah, but when you look back at your life, you realize that it could not have worked out the way it did unless Hashem was running the entire universe.[15]

---

13  *Shemos* 14:30.
14  Ibid. 19:9.
15  A comment from Rabbi Raphael Butler: The Rambam in the *Moreh Nevuchim* (brought by the *Nodeh BeYehudah*) in fact explains that this is "*Shechinah*," the awareness of Hashem through His running the world. The *Mabit* in *Beis Elokim* explains that this is what Chazal mean in מעולם לא זזו שכינה מכותל המערבי. The Midrash *Shir Hashirim Rabbah*, on the *pasuk* of הנה זה עומד אחר כתלינו, says that Hashem made a promise that the Kosel will never be destroyed. Looking back hundreds of years later, we see that this is the case (i.e., we see His clear guiding hand, which is "*Shechinah*"). Although there was never an open miracle on any particular day preventing any Turk or Jordanian etc. from demolishing the Kosel, why didn't they, either today, tomorrow, last week, next month, etc.? It's a *nes* that we see and appreciate only in long-term hindsight.

When you look back on your life, you see that Hashem was there every step of the way. When you look back, courtesy of the Torah and the later history of the Jews, and see how we "met" Hashem, how we distanced Him through our terrible mistakes and how He never abandoned us throughout history, distinguishing us as a holy nation to this very day, you see that Hashem must exist. This, I believe, is what we call the "Holiness of Hashem's Name," His accessibility on earth.

Because of this, we know that He is continuously rescuing us, as He has done constantly in the past—for each of us individually and for Klal Yisrael as a nation. Even if we seem to be facing catastrophe, Hashem always rescues us, whether that rescue comes in this world or the next. "Even if a sharp sword rests on a person's neck, he should not despair of Hashem's mercy."[16]

There is no moment from which it is beyond the ability of Hashem to save us. "*Yeshuas Hashem k'heref ayin*—The salvation of Hashem comes suddenly, in the blink of an eye."[17]

## THE FOURTH BERACHAH: WISDOM AND INSIGHT

אַתָּה חוֹנֵן לְאָדָם דַּעַת וּמְלַמֵּד לֶאֱנוֹשׁ בִּינָה, חָנֵּנוּ מֵאִתְּךָ דֵּעָה בִּינָה וְהַשְׂכֵּל: בָּרוּךְ אַתָּה ה' חוֹנֵן הַדָּעַת:

*You grace man with knowledge and teach understanding to mortals. Grace us from You with wisdom, understanding, and intellect. Blessed are You, Hashem, Who graciously gives wisdom.*

Hashem gave us brains for a reason. Rebbetzin Esther Jungreis used to say, "Some people are so open-minded that their brains fall out."

We are supposed to use our brains to think.

As we discussed earlier, when Jewish men put on tefillin, they first place the tefillin on their arm, next to their heart. Then they place the

---

16  *Berachos* 10a.
17  *Pesikta Zutra* on *Esther* (4:17).

head tefillin on the forehead and then tie the strap of the arm tefillin around their hand.

We can learn from this a basic attitude toward life. Everything begins with the heart. "*Rachamana liba bo'ei*—Hashem desires the heart."[18] We have to train our heart to desire to follow Hashem, to *want* to do good. This can be done.

After the heart, the brain follows, by conceiving a plan of action through which the desire of the heart can be carried out. Then the hand follows; that is the action that completes the process. This is symbolized by the order of putting on tefillin.

The work of the mind, using wisdom and insight, is an essential ingredient for survival. Based on the situation before me, what course of action should I take? The correct decision could spell the difference between not just success and failure, but life and death.

Thus we ask Hashem to bless us with wisdom and insight to pursue the course of action that is going to save us and bring us to redemption.

I am going to add to what I said above about my meeting with former President George W. Bush. It was a miraculous meeting, particularly because I was the only person in a crowd of hundreds to have a personal conversation with the president. Before going to the White House, I asked Hashem for the opportunity to speak to the president, because I wanted to explain how he could do good for the Jews and thereby bring a blessing upon himself and the United States of America.

Among the blessings I gave the president, I said that G-d should give him wisdom and insight to make the right decisions. He appreciated this so much that shortly thereafter, one of his aides came over and thanked me.

We have to know that Hashem gives us the mental tools to help in our own survival. We cannot just rely on Hashem. We have to take an active part on our own behalf. For this, we need the *berachah* of wisdom and insight.

---

18  *Rashi* on *Sanhedrin* 106b.

## THE FIFTH BERACHAH: TESHUVAH

הֲשִׁיבֵנוּ אָבִינוּ לְתוֹרָתֶךָ וְקָרְבֵנוּ מַלְכֵּנוּ לַעֲבוֹדָתֶךָ, וְהַחֲזִירֵנוּ בִּתְשׁוּבָה שְׁלֵמָה לְפָנֶיךָ: בָּרוּךְ אַתָּה ה' הָרוֹצֶה בִּתְשׁוּבָה:

*Return us, our Father, to Your Torah; and bring us close, our King, to Your service; and return us in perfect repentance before You. Blessed are You, Hashem, Who desires repentance.*

Even if we were far away spiritually before, even if we have rebelled against Hashem until now, it is never too late to do *teshuvah*, to repent and ask Him to accept our sincere repentance for running away from Him and doing the wrong things. One of the tactics of the *yetzer hara* is to make us feel hopeless and so deeply mired in bad habits that there is no way out. Depression is one of our worst enemies. We have to know that if we want to come back, Hashem will help us.

In Egypt, Israel fell to the forty-ninth level of impurity. One more degree downward and we would have become indistinguishable from Egyptians and lost our entire unique spiritual heritage. Hashem rescued us at the last moment before we hit bottom, and from there, under the guidance of Moshe Rabbeinu, we climbed back up so that we were actually able to meet Hashem at Har Sinai fifty days later. In the words of Dovid HaMelech, "I am Hashem, your G-d, Who raised you from the land of Egypt."[19]

We have to know that we can recover, even from the very bottom. When the world has gone dark, and we have lost confidence in hope coming from any direction, we should remember that Hashem is above all and can bring us up from the utter depths. We should remember the story of Yosef, who was rushed from prison and instantly became the king of Egypt. The same type of redemption from the depths occurred in the story of Purim. Salvation came instantly and unexpectedly.

---

19   *Vayikra* 11:45 and *Tehillim* 81:11.

"*Yeshuas Hashem k'heref ayin*—the salvation of Hashem comes in the blink of an eye."[20]

"Divine salvation always comes hastily (unexpectedly), as it is written, 'For My salvation is near to come,' and also, 'Oh that My people would hearken to Me…I would soon subdue their enemies'…. And so it will be in the future, as it is written, 'And the Lord whom you seek will suddenly come to His Temple.'"[21]

## THE SIXTH BERACHAH: FORGIVENESS

סְלַח לָנוּ אָבִינוּ כִּי חָטָאנוּ, מְחַל לָנוּ מַלְכֵּנוּ כִּי פָשָׁעְנוּ, כִּי מוֹחֵל וְסוֹלֵחַ אָתָּה: בָּרוּךְ אַתָּה ה' חַנּוּן הַמַּרְבֶּה לִסְלֹחַ:

*Forgive us, our Father, for we have erred; pardon us, our King, for we have willfully sinned; for You pardon and forgive. Blessed are You, Hashem, the Gracious One Who pardons abundantly*

Not only can we repent, but Hashem will forgive us. If He doesn't forgive us, then how can our repentance earn us salvation? We have to know that Hashem actively wants to forgive His children for their mistakes and transgressions. How can we merit being saved if Hashem is not happy with us? We can become terribly depressed because we do not think we are worthy of forgiveness, but Hashem will forgive us if we want to come back to Him. "Comfort, comfort My people, says your G-d."[22]

He will comfort us if we make him "our G-d!"

"Speak to the heart of Yerushalayim and proclaim to her that her time [of exile] has been fulfilled, that her iniquity has been conciliated, for she has received from the hand of Hashem double for all her sins."[23]

Repentance and forgiveness are two different things.

---

20   *Pesikta Zutra* on *Esther* 4:17.
21   *Malachi* 3:1. This entire citation is from the *Seforno* on *Bereishis* 41:14. The Chofetz Chaim on the Torah expresses the same idea.
22   *Yishayah* 40:1; haftarah for *Parashas Va'eschanan*.
23   Ibid.

Repentance is our part: we have to know that we can repent and change our lives. Forgiveness is Hashem's part: we have to know that if we repent, Hashem will accept our repentance, bring us back into favor, and redeem us from "a power mightier than [we]."[24]

## THE SEVENTH BERACHAH: REDEMPTION

רְאֵה בְעָנְיֵנוּ וְרִיבָה רִיבֵנוּ, וּגְאָלֵנוּ מְהֵרָה לְמַעַן שְׁמֶךָ, כִּי גּוֹאֵל חָזָק אָתָּה: בָּרוּךְ אַתָּה ה' גּוֹאֵל יִשְׂרָאֵל:

*Behold our affliction and fight for our causes, and redeem us quickly for the sake of Your Name, for You are a powerful Redeemer. Blessed are You, Hashem, Redeemer of Israel.*

What does "redemption" mean?

Redemption means rescue by Hashem from every situation in which we are trapped. This could be spiritual slavery to our *yetzer hara*. This could be national slavery to our two-thousand-year exile and subjugation to a world that increasingly hates us and tries to impose its poisonous culture upon us. It could also mean personal slavery to torturous conditions of all kinds in which numerous people find themselves trapped.

We need help from Heaven to liberate us on every level.

It is miracle enough when we are able to free ourselves from a constraining force that seems to control us. This is already a miracle, because nothing happens without Hashem making it happen. But when we are freed from a power that is stronger than we are, then we should at once recognize the Hand of Heaven. As we say in the *berachah*, "Hashem has redeemed Yaakov and delivered him from a power mightier than he. Blessed are You Hashem, Who redeemed Israel."

We need to sigh and groan for redemption the way our ancestors did in Egypt! Are we feeling the servitude of exile? Are we attributing our troubles to exile?

---

24  *Maariv.*

> *During those many days, it happened that the king of Egypt died, and B'nei Yisrael groaned because of the work, and they cried out. Their outcry because of the work went up to Hashem. Hashem heard their moaning and Hashem remembered His covenant with Avraham, with Yitzchak, and with Yaakov. Hashem saw B'nei Yisrael and Hashem knew.*[25]

In order to save ourselves, we have to want to be saved. Today, although existence is clearly becoming more dangerous throughout the world, it doesn't seem that we are "groaning" and "crying out" very much. In general, Jews are living good lives in accordance with the general prosperity that still exists in the world. In many countries, Jews have plenty of food, political power, beautiful homes, vacations, and leisure time to enjoy numerous luxuries. There is much anguish and tragedy and there are many dark clouds appearing on the horizon, but it seems that many people try not to think about it.

This is ominously reminiscent of the period before many terrible tragedies. In Egypt itself, many from B'nei Yisrael assimilated into Egyptian culture. *Rashi* asserts that four-fifths of B'nei Yisrael never left Egypt, having perished in *Makkas Choshech* because they did not want to follow Moshe out of Egypt. "Why did [Hashem] bring [the plague of] darkness against them? There were among Israel of that generation wicked individuals who did not wish to depart [from Egypt] and they died during the three days of darkness."[26] "It is well-known that the Israelites in Egypt were exceedingly wicked and sinful, and they abrogated also the [commandment of] circumcision."[27]

This is staggering, but history repeats itself. Before the days of Hitler, may his memory be ground to dust, Germany was the place in which the evil of assimilation flowered, threatening to take over the entire Jewish community. People began to think that Berlin was Yerushalayim![28]

---

25  *Shemos* 2:23–25.
26  *Rashi* to *Shemos* 10:22.
27  *Ramban* on *Shemos* 12:42.
28  *Meshech Chochmah*.

> *Nineteenth-century European society opened its doors to the Jew, and, for the first time since the Karaites, non-observance as an organized movement, complete with leaders, ideology, and literature, became a reality in Jewish life. Rabbi [Samson Raphael] Hirsch [in Germany] was the first European gadol to set forth a comprehensive Torah response to this institutionalized heresy.*[29]

Despite the heroic struggles of the great rabbis of the time, this organized attack against classic Torah observance was the beginning of the end of the old order of Jewish life in the European exile. The obvious countdown to the final redemption began with the First World War, which destroyed the world of the *shtetl*.

Rabbi Elchonen Wasserman stated:

> *Immediately after the First World War, I heard from the Chofetz Chaim that the War of Gog and Magog will be split into three parts. The first part is the war (World War I) that just passed. The second will be in another twenty-five to thirty years. [Indeed, World War II began exactly twenty-five years after the outbreak of World War I.] After that will be the third and final war, and then the final redemption. The Chofetz Chaim added that, in the third war, the entire world will suffer from the "birth pangs of Moshiach."*[30]

"[The] Israelites [because of their sins] were not deserving to be redeemed…except that [Hashem] accepted their outcry and their moaning because of the great pain they were in…."[31] We must take our danger seriously enough to cry out, "moaning," to Hashem.

---

29  *Rabbi Samson Raphael Hirsch*, Arscroll/Mesorah, Preface, p. xii.
30  Quoted in *Redemption Unfolding*, page 90ff.
31  *Ramban* on *Shemos* 12:42.

## THE EIGHTH BERACHAH: HEALTH AND HEALING

רְפָאֵנוּ ה' וְנֵרָפֵא הוֹשִׁיעֵנוּ וְנִוָּשֵׁעָה כִּי תְהִלָּתֵנוּ אָתָּה, וְהַעֲלֵה רְפוּאָה שְׁלֵמָה לְכָל מַכּוֹתֵינוּ, כִּי אֵ-ל מֶלֶךְ רוֹפֵא נֶאֱמָן וְרַחֲמָן אָתָּה: בָּרוּךְ אַתָּה ה' רוֹפֵא חוֹלֵי עַמּוֹ יִשְׂרָאֵל:

*Heal us, Hashem; then we will be healed. Save us; then we will be saved, for You are our praise. Bring complete recovery for all our ailments, for You are the Almighty King, the faithful and compassionate Healer. Blessed are You, Hashem, Who heals the sick of His people Israel.*

One of the dangers of the culture of Edom is that we place our trust in technology and not in Hashem. This is certainly true in the field of medicine. With the tremendous development of modern medicine, which has benefited humanity incredibly, one can easily come to believe that the healer is the doctor or the medicine, and not the Master of the World. There is a special *tefillah* to say before taking medicine, in which we acknowledge that Hashem is the One Who gives and sustains life.

There is much sickness in the world today. There are strange diseases and many tragedies, some of which seem to have arisen because of modern medicine itself, like diseases that arise in hospitals, or bacteria that are resistant to antibiotics.

There is also intentional violence, people acting in a hostile manner and inflicting damage on others. In addition, the world is not clean: the air, fresh water, and the oceans are polluted. The world is drowning in plastic and other refuse that cannot decompose. The planet is becoming increasingly unhealthy. Many species of plant and animal are becoming extinct because mankind is poisoning the earth.

Even some varieties of common fruits and vegetables, including bananas, apples, and coffee beans, are in danger of extinction.[32] Modern growing methods and export requirements have caused growers to reduce the varieties of plants they cultivate. When those fewer varieties

---

32   This is not an exaggeration. See reports in *Hamodia's Binyan Magazine*, February 13, 2019; CNN, January 8, 2016; *New York Post*, January 17, 2019; BBC, April 1, 2014.

are attacked by disease or insects, there are few alternative varieties left to cultivate. International travel is also bringing alien species into vulnerable environments, further endangering the food supply.

When plant and animal species die out, the entire world structure is shaken to the core. Hashem made the world with infinite care and knowledge. When one facet of creation is destroyed, the entire structure suffers. As the midrash tells us, "Every blade of grass has an angel that stands by it and says, 'Grow!'" [33]

Dovid HaMelech says, "The heavens will be glad and the earth will rejoice. The sea and its fullness will roar. The field and everything in it will exult. Then all the trees of the forest will sing with joy before Hashem for He will have arrived. He will have arrived to judge the earth." [34]

Why will the earth rejoice when the redemption comes?

"The sea and its fullness will roar; the inhabited land and those who dwell therein; rivers will clap hands, mountains will exult together before Hashem, for He will have arrived to judge the earth. He will judge the world with righteousness and peoples with fairness." [35]

Why will rivers clap hands?

This is an amazing affirmation of what will be in the days after the Final Redemption. The earth will rejoice! The trees of the forest will sing! They will have been rescued from the destructive force of mankind, a civilization that is exploiting the perfect world that Hashem created.

Esav's first recorded words were, "Pour into me, now, some of that very red stuff....." [36] This is Esav: "I must eat! Pour it down my throat! Now!" His ravenous descendants are threatening the world environment.

We need Hashem's mercy to heal us and save our world.

## THE NINTH BERACHAH: A YEAR OF PROSPERITY

בָּרֵךְ עָלֵינוּ ה' אֱ-לֹהֵינוּ אֶת הַשָּׁנָה הַזֹּאת וְאֶת כָּל מִינֵי תְבוּאָתָהּ
לְטוֹבָה, וְתֵן (בקיץ: בְּרָכָה) (בחורף: טַל וּמָטָר לִבְרָכָה) עַל פְּנֵי

---

33  *Midrash Rabbah, Bereishis* 10:6.
34  *Tehillim* 96.
35  Ibid. 98.
36  *Bereishis* 25:30.

הָאֲדָמָה, וְשַׂבְּעֵנוּ מִטּוּבָהּ, וּבָרֵךְ שְׁנָתֵנוּ כַּשָּׁנִים הַטּוֹבוֹת: בָּרוּךְ אַתָּה ה' מְבָרֵךְ הַשָּׁנִים:

> *Bless on our behalf, Hashem our G-d, this year and all its various crops for goodness, and give (dew and rain for a) blessing on the face of the earth, and satisfy us from Your bounty, and bless our year like the best years. Blessed are You, Hashem, Who blesses the years.*

This is a *berachah* for prosperity, for crops, for material sustenance, for profitable business. We need the constant blessing of Hashem in order to survive physically. Following our expulsion from Gan Eden, we require "*zei'as apecha*—the sweat of your brow"[37] in order to obtain our food and sustenance. "The sweat of your brow" may also refer to the mental anguish that frequently accompanies earning one's livelihood.

I believe that this *berachah* refers especially to the Land of Israel, even more than the lands of our exile, because the sustenance we obtain from the Land of Israel is dependent completely on the prayers and behavior of Klal Yisrael.

In other lands, rains come through the normal course of nature; the climate follows an expected pattern. In London, it rains almost half the days of the year, but some parts of the Sahara Desert receive less than one inch of rain per year. In Egypt, the Nile River floods annually and irrigates the ground.

But the blessings in the Land of Israel are completely dependent upon our supplications to Hashem.

> *For the land to which you come, to possess it, it is not like the land of Egypt that you left, where you would plant your seed and water it on foot like a vegetable garden. But the land to which you cross over to possess it is a land of mountains and valleys. From the rain of heaven it drinks water, a land that Hashem your G-d, seeks out. The eyes of Hashem, your*

---

37   Ibid. 3:19.

G-d, are always upon it, from the beginning of the year to year's end.[38]

Every day in the *Shema* we say:

*It will be that, if you hearken to My commandments that I command you today, to love Hashem your G-d and to serve Him with all your heart and with all your soul, then I shall provide rain for your land in its proper time, the early and the late rains, that you may gather in your grain, your wine, and your oil. I shall provide grass in your field for your cattle, and you will eat and you will be satisfied.*[39]

Eretz Yisrael is the place in which there is the most direct connection between whether we "hearken to [His] commandments" and the provision of our material sustenance.

Thus, every year, during Pesach, we daven for *tal*, dew, and we beg Hashem, "Give dew to favor Your land, to establish us for blessing [and] to re-establish the City which is Your delight."[40]

And then, during Sukkos, we daven for rain. "Af-Bri is designated as the name of the angel of rain, to thicken and to form clouds, to empty them out and to cause rain, providing water to bring the vegetation with which the valleys will be crowned…."[41]

Of course, we need to daven in other lands, but Eretz Yisrael is the land of *ruchniyus*, and it is sustained through the spiritual level of Klal Yisrael. That is why we are exiled from the land—G-d forbid!—when we fall below the proper *madreigah*.

*Beware for yourselves, lest your heart be seduced and you turn astray and serve gods of others and bow to them, then the wrath of Hashem shall blaze against you, and He will restrain the heaven so that there will not be rain and the ground will*

---

38  *Devarim* 11:10.
39  Ibid. 11:13–15.
40  *Tefillas Tal*.
41  *Tefillas Geshem*.

> *not yield its produce, and you will be banished swiftly from upon the goodly land which Hashem gives you!*[42]

When I say this *berachah*, I think particularly about how the Land of Israel needs both Jews and Torah in order to flourish. The covenant between Hashem and Avraham Avinu established the eternal link between the people and the land and the Torah. As Hashem promises, "I will give to you and to your offspring after you the land of your sojourns, the whole of the land of Canaan as an everlasting possession, and I shall be a G-d to them."[43]

I am emotional about this *berachah*, because I think about how the land itself is crying out for Torah. The land is crying for Shabbos! The land is crying out for *shemittah*! The land is crying out for *terumos* and *ma'asros*!

When will Torah come to the Land of Israel? When will we return to sanity? When will we stop fighting with those who love Torah? The Land of Israel needs to be cleaned up spiritually. How can we expect blessing when we rebel against the One Who provides all blessing? This is true especially in the Holy Land! How can we expect protection when we insult the One Who protects us, the Guardian of Israel, "Who neither slumbers nor sleeps!"[44]

The plea for dew and rain is contained in this prayer. In many recent years, the Land of Israel has suffered from insufficient rain. The Kinneret sank dangerously low. Winter should be the time of rain, but in many recent years the rains did not fall in sufficient quantity to sustain the water supply. One of the most magnificent sights in Israel is Mount Hermon covered in snow, but some years the snow does not fall.

As we saw above, Hashem has warned us: "Beware lest your heart be seduced and you turn astray and serve gods of others and bow to them. The wrath of Hashem will blaze against you. He will restrain the heaven so there will be no rain and the ground will not yield its produce...."[45]

---

42  *Devarim* 11:16ff.
43  *Bereishis* 17:8.
44  *Tehillim* 121.
45  *Devarim* 11:16.

My friends, could it be clearer than that? We say this twice every day! It is all there, in black and white. If we serve Hashem properly, we will have every blessing.

And what about our enemies? It is quite clear that the world is against us. On what basis do we deserve to be in the Holy Land? "Not because you are more numerous than all the other peoples did Hashem desire you and choose you, for you are the fewest of all the peoples."[46]

We are the smallest nation! How can we survive amidst enemies who outnumber us by the billions? The people and the Land of Israel can survive only if we are completely dedicated to our Creator. "Praise Hashem, all nations, extol Him, all the states. For His kindness overwhelms us, and the truth of Hashem is eternal."[47] Nothing can stand in the way of His will. But we have to try to deserve His blessings.

## THE TENTH BERACHAH: THE INGATHERING OF THE EXILES

תְּקַע בְּשׁוֹפָר גָּדוֹל לְחֵרוּתֵנוּ, וְשָׂא נֵס לְקַבֵּץ גָּלֻיּוֹתֵינוּ, וְקַבְּצֵנוּ יַחַד מֵאַרְבַּע כַּנְפוֹת הָאָרֶץ: בָּרוּךְ אַתָּה ה' מְקַבֵּץ נִדְחֵי עַמּוֹ יִשְׂרָאֵל:

*Sound the great shofar for our freedom; raise the banner to gather our exiles, and gather us together from the four corners of the earth. Blessed are You, Hashem, Who gathers in the dispersed of His people Israel.*

The language of this *berachah* is amazing. We are asking Hashem to let us hear the *shofar gadol*, the sound we have been waiting to hear since the beginning of our history, the sound that will tell the entire world that Moshiach has come. We want to hear it, and we should tell Hashem we want to hear it.

The *berachah* asks Hashem to send a *nes*. This word is frequently translated as "miracle," but it literally means "sign" or "banner." We are begging Hashem to gather all the exiles, the entire family of Israel, from

---

46   Ibid. 7:7.
47   *Tehillim* 117.

the "four corners" of the earth. It is not explicitly stated, but clearly, we are being gathered together to return to our Holy Land of Israel.

We are asking for signs that are going to be understood around the world. At that time, there will be no doubt about what is happening.

There will be no politics, no electioneering, no popularity polls!

When the great *shofar* sounds, this sign will be recognized by everyone!

No longer will people vie for votes and power. No longer will bitter politics and blaring headlines bring anger and divisiveness.

No! The world will be united. The word of Hashem will be supreme.

"*Ki miTziyon teitzei Torah u'd'var Hashem miYerushalayim*—the Torah will go forth from Tziyon and the word of Hashem from Yerushalayim."[48] It will be clear that there is One Ruler, and His king will indisputably represent the King of the Universe.

There will be unity and peace in the world and Hashem's Presence will be palpable. "*Hashem echad u'Shemo echad*—He will be one and His Name one,"[49] meaning that the proponents of idolatry will no longer claim that their idols have any reality. As we say, "All the gods of the peoples are nothings! But Hashem made heaven."[50] This is what we are praying for when we say this *berachah*.

## THE ELEVENTH BERACHAH: RESTORATION OF JUSTICE

הָשִׁיבָה שׁוֹפְטֵינוּ כְּבָרִאשׁוֹנָה וְיוֹעֲצֵינוּ כְּבַתְּחִלָּה וְהָסֵר מִמֶּנּוּ יָגוֹן וַאֲנָחָה, וּמְלֹךְ עָלֵינוּ אַתָּה ה' לְבַדְּךָ בְּחֶסֶד וּבְרַחֲמִים, וְצַדְּקֵנוּ בַּמִּשְׁפָּט: בָּרוּךְ אַתָּה ה' מֶלֶךְ אוֹהֵב צְדָקָה וּמִשְׁפָּט:

*Restore our judges as in earliest times and our counselors as at first; remove from us sorrow and groaning, and reign over us, You, Hashem, alone, with kindness and compassion, and justify us through judgement. Blessed are You, Hashem, the King Who loves righteousness and judgment.*

---

48   *Yeshayah* 2:3.
49   *Devarim* 6:4.
50   *Divrei Hayamim I* 16:26.

When Moshiach comes, the world will be stable. We need to live in a stable environment, where the beastly inclination of man does not prevail. "Pray for the welfare of the government, because if people did not fear it, a person would swallow his fellow alive."[51]

Not long ago I was driving in a suburban residential community, on a main street, about to turn onto a smaller street. A car was approaching the intersection. At that moment, I was slowing down to make the turn. There was a stop sign for the oncoming car, but the driver went through the stop sign. I was now straight in front of him, maybe six feet away, and he was headed directly at me. He was not moving fast, but he was moving. I sounded the horn, thinking he had not seen me. But he had seen me. Despite that, he kept coming, moving forward. He was moving slowly, but he was moving, and I was right in front of him. He just kept moving, making it difficult for me to turn, because he was now probably two to three feet away from me. But he didn't stop; he just kept going forward.

What I am describing was intentional, malicious, provocative, confrontational, aggressive, and gratuitous. There was no reason for him to keep going. He knew exactly what he was doing. It represented a meaningless and gratuitous desire to pick a fight. Unfortunately, I believe the world is filled with such aggressive, contentious, and dangerous people.

Do we have righteous judges and public officials today? Is there somewhere, anywhere, that is operating according to the laws of the Torah?

Before the *Mabul*, the Torah tells us that "Hashem saw that the wickedness of man was great upon the earth, and that every product of the thoughts of his heart was but evil always."[52]

This *berachah* asks that Hashem "restore our judges as in earliest times and our counselors as at first." These phrases refer to the days when the Sanhedrin ruled in Israel and the prophets guided our nation.

There is no justice unless it takes its direction from the Torah. There is no stability unless it is the stability of the Torah. "[Hashem] suspends

---

51   *Pirkei Avos* 3:2.
52   *Bereishis* 6:5.

the earth upon nothingness."[53] Everything in this universe exists only because Hashem wills it to exist.

Do you remember the amazing quotation from President Harry S. Truman? This is what he said, "I believe that just like in the past, three thousand years ago, you Jews saved humanity, wild mankind, via your Torah; so too, I believe and hope that even nowadays, you, the Jewish Nation, will be successful again, to enlighten and to heal the beasts of cruelty in our midst and save the world from total destruction."

## THE TWELFTH BERACHAH: AGAINST HERETICS

וְלַמַּלְשִׁינִים אַל תְּהִי תִקְוָה, וְכָל הָרִשְׁעָה כְּרֶגַע תֹּאבֵד, וְכָל אוֹיְבֶיךָ מְהֵרָה יִכָּרֵתוּ, וְהַזֵּדִים מְהֵרָה תְעַקֵּר וּתְשַׁבֵּר וּתְמַגֵּר וְתַכְנִיעַ בִּמְהֵרָה בְיָמֵינוּ: בָּרוּךְ אַתָּה ה' שׁוֹבֵר אוֹיְבִים וּמַכְנִיעַ זֵדִים:

*And for slanderers let there be no hope; and may all wickedness perish in an instant; and may all Your enemies be cut down speedily. May You speedily uproot, smash, cast down, and humble the wanton sinners, speedily in our days. Blessed are You, Hashem, Who breaks enemies and humbles wanton sinners.*

Unfortunately, there are people today who are actively trying to undermine the Torah. They are the enemies of G-d and man. There were Jewish *"kapos"*[54] in ancient Egypt and in the modern Holocaust, Jews who thought there would be a personal advantage in working as enemies of their own people. And since the days of Moshe, there have been enemies within our ranks, such as Korach, who slandered Moshe and tried to depose him.

Here is what the late Rabbi Avigdor Miller says about Jews who became enemies of their own people:

---

53   *Iyov* 26:7.
54   A *kapo* was a Jewish prisoner who acted as a guard in the Nazi concentration camps.

*During the past century, the ranks of [Gentile] slanderers have been swelled by pen-wielders and orators from our own people. Poems, satires, malicious novels, prejudiced history books, and propaganda literature have poured from the presses of the Maskilim, the Socialists, the Bundists, the Communists, the Reformers and renegades from Judaism operating as freelancers in their own name. So much odium was cast on the name of true Judaism that many were ashamed to admit their loyalty to Torah. An Orthodox Jew was something to sneer at, at best to tolerate, but never to admire. The profaning of the laws of the Torah became a matter of course. Under the smoke barrage of the newspapers and orators, the common people were enabled to divest themselves without embarrassment of their former responsibilities. The prejudice against Torah was established, after years of propaganda, in the common people.*[55]

These are the people whose legacy in Europe was the rise of Nazism. We have to know that Hashem's tolerance for such people will reach a limit beyond which He will not go, as the Torah clearly demonstrates in the case of Korach: "The earth opened its mouth and swallowed [Dasan and Aviram] and their households and all the people who were with Korach and their entire wealth. They and all that was theirs descended alive to the pit; the earth covered them over and they were lost from among the congregation…A flame came forth from Hashem and consumed the two hundred and fifty men who were offering the incense."[56]

## THE THIRTEENTH BERACHAH: THE RIGHTEOUS

עַל הַצַּדִּיקִים וְעַל הַחֲסִידִים וְעַל זִקְנֵי עַמְּךָ בֵּית יִשְׂרָאֵל וְעַל פְּלֵיטַת סוֹפְרֵיהֶם וְעַל גֵּרֵי הַצֶּדֶק וְעָלֵינוּ, יֶהֱמוּ רַחֲמֶיךָ ה' אֱ-לֹהֵינוּ, וְתֵן שָׂכָר טוֹב לְכָל הַבּוֹטְחִים בְּשִׁמְךָ בֶּאֱמֶת, וְשִׂים

---

55 Rabbi Avigdor Miller, *A Divine Madness*, pp. 31–32.
56 *Vayikra* 16:32ff.

חֶלְקֵנוּ עִמָּהֶם לְעוֹלָם וְלֹא נֵבוֹשׁ כִּי בְךָ בָטָחְנוּ: בָּרוּךְ אַתָּה ה'
מִשְׁעָן וּמִבְטָח לַצַּדִּיקִים:

> *On the righteous, on the devout, on the elders of Your people the Family of Israel, on the remnant of their scholars, on the righteous converts and on ourselves, may Your mercy be aroused, Hashem, our G-d, and give goodly reward to all who sincerely trust in Your Name. Place our portion with them forever, and we will not be ashamed, for we trust in You. Blessed are You, Hashem, Supporter and Provider of assurance for the righteous.*

Thank G-d, there are righteous people in the world.

Even though Dovid HaMelech says, "The devout one is no more, for truthful men have vanished from mankind,"[57] hidden away in this world there must be a few righteous people who sustain it, because otherwise the world would cease to exist.

How are we supposed to act?

- "The world exists only on account of [the humility of] Moshe and Aharon."[58] They are our role models for proper behavior.
- Hashem spoke to Eliyahu with a "still, thin sound."[59] Hashem shows us that people who scream cannot be trusted.
- "The world exists only on account of one who muzzles himself at a time of provocation [and refrains from reacting]."[60]

People who desire a clean, righteous, and pure world in which the laws of Hashem prevail must not give up hope, even though the world all around us is crumbling morally and physically. We are able to derive hope and direction from our Avos and Imahos, who also lived in a debased world given over to idolatry.

As the first *berachah* in *Shemoneh Esreh* tells us, Hashem provided a *magen*, a shield that protected Avraham, and we pray that this shield

---

57  *Tehillim* 12.
58  *Chullin* 89a.
59  *Melachim I* 19:12.
60  *Chullin* 89a.

will protect us as well. Today, when the world is filled with immorality, violence, insane ideas, and insane people, we have to know that we are still able to cling to Hashem and His Torah. Those who deny the existence of Hashem are trying to push Him out of His own world. In His mercy, He waits for them to repent, but it seems that time is running very short.

The language of this *berachah* is amazing. In Hebrew, the word for "security" is *"bitachon."* This *berachah* says that the hallmark of a righteous person is that he clings to Hashem. Even when the world is spinning out of control, we can cling to Hashem.

> *On the righteous, on the devout, on the elders of Your people, the family of Israel, on the remnant of their scholars...may Your compassion be aroused.... Give a goodly reward to all who sincerely believe in Your Name. Put our lot with them forever and we will not feel ashamed, for we trust [and here the word is "betachnu"—we have bitachon] in You.*[61]

If we cling to Hashem, then we are constantly coming nearer to Him. We have a direction in life. We are traveling toward Hashem. Sometimes we may veer away but we can always correct our course. "Many are the mishaps of the righteous, but from them all Hashem rescues him."[62]

Dovid HaMelech says, "In the evening, one lies down weeping, but, with dawn, a cry of joy!"[63]

This is the story of life. We are in darkness, and we are looking for light. If we know it is there, then we will continue to search for it.

"The Rock! His work is perfect, for all His paths are justice, a Hashem of faith without iniquity; righteous and fair."[64]

We have to know there is such a path, even when the world seems totally black.

---

61  Language of the *berachah*.
62  *Tehillim* 34.
63  Ibid. 30.
64  *Devarim* 32:4.

I am writing these very words on the second day of Chanukah in the year 5779 (December 2018). Chanukah is the archetypal holiday of exile. It occurs during the darkest season of the year, when the nights are long and the days are short. It is the only holiday that occurs at the end of the Jewish month, when the moon is fading and finally disappears altogether from the night sky. It is the absolute darkest moment of the year.

What do we do on Chanukah? We light our own lights. We bring light into the darkness and do not let the darkness envelop us. And what does Hashem do to respond to the light we bring into His world? He brings a new moon. By the eighth day of Chanukah, there is always a thin crescent moon in the sky, and that crescent will grow. Hashem will send light into the world in response to the light we bring.

As we say in *Kiddush Levanah*, "May it be Your will, Hashem…to fill the flaw of the moon that there be no diminution in it. May the light of the moon be like the light of the sun and like the light of the seven days of Creation, as it was before it was diminished, as it is said, 'The two great luminaries….'"

## THE FOURTEENTH BERACHAH: REBUILDING YERUSHALAYIM

וְלִירוּשָׁלַיִם עִירְךָ בְּרַחֲמִים תָּשׁוּב וְתִשְׁכֹּן בְּתוֹכָהּ כַּאֲשֶׁר דִּבַּרְתָּ, וּבְנֵה אוֹתָהּ בְּקָרוֹב בְּיָמֵינוּ בִּנְיַן עוֹלָם, וְכִסֵּא דָוִד מְהֵרָה לְתוֹכָהּ תָּכִין: בָּרוּךְ אַתָּה ה' בּוֹנֵה יְרוּשָׁלָיִם:

*And to Yerushalayim, Your city, may You return in mercy, and may You dwell within it as You have spoken. May You rebuild it soon in our days as an eternal structure, and may You speedily establish the throne of David within it. Blessed are You, Hashem, the Builder of Yerushalayim.*

Do you think that modern-day Yerushalayim is the Yerushalayim that we are praying for?

We are praying and working for and expecting perfection. Yerushalayim in the time of Moshiach will be dedicated to the service of Hashem, with no rebellion against Torah and no friction among Klal Yisrael. There will be no moral or physical pollution. There will be no demonstrations by people who are trying to overturn the Torah. Yerushalayim will be built around the Beis Hamikdash, and the King's majesty will embrace His people and draw them close. The city will be filled with *yiras Shamayim*, the awe of Hashem, and *ahavas Yisrael*, brotherly love. The nations will no longer covet Yerushalayim because they will know that it belongs to the Jews and the awe of us will be upon them.

"In the future, the Holy One, blessed be He, will bring precious stones and pearls that are thirty *amos* by thirty *amos* and will cut out from them [an opening] ten [*amos* wide] by twenty [*amos*] high, and He will install them [as] the gates of Yerushalayim."[65]

We should cry while reciting this *berachah*.

Holy people know how to cry. "Then Yosef rushed because his compassion for his brother had been stirred and he wanted to weep; so he went into the room and wept there."[66] "Anyone who mourns over Yerushalayim is deserving to witness her joy."[67]

This is something we have to feel. If we cannot cry over the pain, we should cry over the fact that we do not feel the pain. Dovid HaMelech, the ancestor of Moshiach, also knew how to cry. "Every night I drench my bed; with my tears I soak my couch...."[68]

The *Shema* begins with the words, "You shall love Hashem your G-d with all your heart and with all your soul and with all your resources...."[69]

How can we love Hashem with all our heart if we do not feel emotional when we are davening? When we beg Hashem to rebuild Yerushalayim, how can we not be upset that there is a secular government running the Holy City—and all of Israel—and so many of our people are alienated from our Torah? How can we not cry about this?

---

65  *Sanhedrin* 100a. An *amah* is approximately twenty inches, so an opening of twenty *amos* would be somewhat less than twenty feet high.
66  *Bereishis* 43:30.
67  *Taanis* 30b.
68  *Tehillim* 6.
69  *Devarim* 6:5.

If we cry, then I believe that we have an assurance that Hashem will help us. As Dovid HaMelech says, "You have delivered my soul from death [and] my eyes from tears."[70]

Every human faculty plays a part in coming home to Hashem. When it comes to Yerushalayim, we really have to cry.

> *By the rivers of Babylon, there we sat and also wept when we remembered Tziyon. On the willows within it we hung our lyres. There our captors requested words of song from us, with our lyres playing joyous music. "Sing for us from Tziyon's song." How can we sing the song of Hashem upon the alien's soil? If I forget you, O Yerushalayim, let my right hand forget its skill. Let my tongue adhere to my palate if I fail to recall you, if I fail to elevate Yerushalayim above my foremost joy....*[71]

## THE FIFTEENTH BERACHAH: MOSHIACH

אֶת צֶמַח דָּוִד עַבְדְּךָ מְהֵרָה תַצְמִיחַ, וְקַרְנוֹ תָּרוּם בִּישׁוּעָתֶךָ, כִּי לִישׁוּעָתְךָ קִוִּינוּ כָּל הַיּוֹם: בָּרוּךְ אַתָּה ה' מַצְמִיחַ קֶרֶן יְשׁוּעָה:

*May You quickly cause the offspring of Your servant David to flourish, and raise his pride through Your salvation, for we hope for Your salvation all day long. Blessed are You, Hashem, Who causes the pride of salvation to flourish.*

Do you know how this *berachah* asks for Moshiach? It ends with the words, "*matzmiach keren yeshuah.*" According to my understanding, this means that we are asking Hashem to enable the "horn of salvation" to grow. What is the "horn of salvation?" The word for horn is *keren*, and I believe it literally means the horn of an animal. In order to anoint a king, they would take the hollowed-out horn of an animal, fill it with oil, and place that oil on the king's forehead.

---

70  *Tehillim* 116.
71  Ibid. 137.

When Shmuel HaNavi came to anoint Dovid king over Israel, he brought his horn and filled it with oil. "Hashem said to Shmuel, 'How long will you mourn over Shaul when I have rejected him from reigning over Israel? Fill your horn with oil and go forth. I shall send you to Yishai from Beis Lechem, for I have seen a king for myself among his sons....'"[72]

When Dovid appeared before Shmuel, "Hashem said, 'Arise and anoint him, for this is he!' Samuel took the horn of oil and anointed him in the midst of his brothers, and the spirit of Hashem passed over Dovid from that day on."[73]

From many places in Yerushalayim, one can see the tomb of Shmuel HaNavi. When I am in Yerushalayim, I try to look at that holy site every day. I ask Hashem to please send the prophet who will stand in the place of Shmuel and anoint Moshiach, the descendant of Dovid HaMelech, soon in our days. What we need is not someone who wins an election filled with strife and acrimony, but someone who—like Dovid HaMelech—is selected by Hashem to lead the people of Israel. Since Israel is the nation chosen to lead the entire world in obedience to Hashem, the leader of Israel will in fact be the leader of the entire world.

> *The Sages and prophets did not yearn for the Messianic era in order to have dominion over the entire world to rule over the gentiles, to be exalted by the nations, or to eat, drink, and celebrate. Rather [they desired] to be free [to involve themselves] in Torah and wisdom without any pressures or disturbances, so that they would merit the World to Come.... In that era...the occupation of the entire world will be solely to know Hashem...as [the Navi] states:[74] "The world will be filled with the knowledge of Hashem as the waters cover the ocean bed."[75]*

---

72  *Shmuel I* 16:1ff.
73  Ibid 16:12ff.
74  *Yeshayah* 11:9.
75  *Rambam, Hilchos Melachim* 12:4–5.

This is how Dovid HaMelech himself expresses it: "*Achas sha'alti*—One thing I asked of Hashem, that I shall seek: To dwell in the House of Hashem all the days of my life, to behold the sweetness of Hashem and to contemplate in His Sanctuary...."[76]

## THE SIXTEENTH BERACHAH: ACCEPTANCE OF PRAYER

שְׁמַע קוֹלֵנוּ ה' אֱ-לֹהֵינוּ, חוּס וְרַחֵם עָלֵינוּ וְקַבֵּל בְּרַחֲמִים וּבְרָצוֹן אֶת תְּפִלָּתֵנוּ, כִּי אֵ-ל שׁוֹמֵעַ תְּפִלּוֹת וְתַחֲנוּנִים אָתָּה, וּמִלְּפָנֶיךָ מַלְכֵּנוּ רֵיקָם אַל תְּשִׁיבֵנוּ, כִּי אַתָּה שׁוֹמֵעַ תְּפִלַּת עַמְּךָ יִשְׂרָאֵל בְּרַחֲמִים: בָּרוּךְ אַתָּה ה' שׁוֹמֵעַ תְּפִלָּה.

> *Hear our voice, Hashem, our G-d; pity and be merciful to us, and accept with mercy and favor our prayer, for You are the Almighty Who hears prayers and entreaties. Do not turn us away empty-handed from before You, our King, for You hear the prayer of Your people Israel with mercy. Blessed are You, Hashem, Who hears prayer.*

Here, in a sense, we ratify the entire process, meaning that we certify that we believe in the power of prayer and ask that Hashem accept our prayers and guide us in the right direction. I believe that we are also asking Hashem to enable us to pray for the right things. It is no good if we pray for the wrong things. One has to know what to ask for.

People say to others, "May your prayers be answered."

But wait a minute…. How do you know you want this person's prayers to be answered? How do you know what that person is praying for? Do you want an evil person's prayers to be answered? Evil people also ask Hashem to answer their prayers.

"Balak, son of Zippor, saw all that Israel had done…. He sent messengers to Bilaam, son of Beor…to summon him, saying…'Please come and curse this people [Israel] for me….'"[77] Bilaam was aware of Hashem's existence, but he wanted Hashem to curse and not bless us.

---

76  *Tehillim* 27.
77  *Numbers* 22:2ff.

Our prayers must be correct, articulate, and straight.

That is the beauty of the order of the prayers established by our Avos and then formulated in the current order by the *Anshei Knesses Hagedolah*, who composed, with Divine assistance, the order of prayer that we say today and have said for thousands of years since. These prayers have literally enabled us to survive through our cruel and torturous dispersion to the ends of the earth.

What is the *Anshei Knesses Hagedolah*?

> *Anshei Knesses Hagedolah, the Men of the Great Assembly, was founded by Ezra approximately 2,500 years ago. This institution of Torah Sages led the Jewish People at the beginning of the Second Temple Era. It included Mordechai and the last of the prophets, Chaggai, Zecharyah, and Malachi. Among [their] accomplishments…were finalizing the contents of the Tanach, instituting the Shemoneh Esreh prayer and enacting laws to protect and bolster the observance of Torah.*
>
> *There was a sense among the great rabbis of the time that the Second Temple would not last, because the Divine Presence was not as concentrated as it had been in the First Temple, and it would be necessary to prepare the people for a long, uncharted journey in exile, with only the guiding but unseen "Hand of Hashem" and His "Eyes," watching from "behind the curtain."*
>
> *This institution was called "great" because it "restored the crown of the Torah," served as the spiritual center of Jewish life [before the churban Bayis Sheini, and thus] ensured the survival of the Jewish People through the coming harsh conditions of the [coming] exile.*[78]

The *Anshei Knesses Hagedolah* kept alive the greatness of Am Yisrael and the Torah of Israel during the incredibly degrading conditions of destruction and exile. They emphasized the miracles through which

---

78    Statement composed by the Orthodox Union, February 7, 2014.

Torah culture survived. "If not for the awe of [the nations] for the Holy One, blessed be He, how could one [solitary] nation survive among the [seventy hateful] nations [of the world]?"[79]

"The same sentiment is captured in an exchange between Rabbi Yehoshua and the Emperor Hadrian reported in *Midrash Tanchuma*.... Hadrian said to Rabbi Yehoshua, 'How great is the lamb that survives among the seventy wolves!' [Rabbi Yehoshua] replied: 'How great is the Shepherd Who protects her!'"[80]

We owe the *Anshei Knesses Hagedolah* everlasting gratitude for composing these prayers and practices that have guided and sustained us, individually and nationally, in our agonizing exile until this very day. This is nothing less than our umbilical cord to Hashem, the open door to communication with the King of the Universe.

Modern man thinks he understands the universe, but the universe he understands is only a creation of the King of Kings, and modern man has no clue to what is behind the physical world in which Hashem has placed us.

We think we are intelligent, but we are misled! The world is sure that they know everything, but their eyes are blinded by their desire to exclude Hashem from the world.

"That is what *Kabbalas haTorah* (receiving the Torah from Hashem at Har Sinai) really meant: We give up our own thoughts, our baby thoughts, and we rise to the thoughts of the Supreme Intelligence and think His thoughts. And those are the attitudes and ideals that we adopt as our own..."[81]

Indeed, perhaps the biggest problem in history is that we think we know more than Hashem. That is what happened with Chavah and then Adam in Gan Eden, and it is happening to this day. We think we know everything, but we really know nothing. We think we are building a technological paradise, but in fact we are destroying the world.

---

79  *Yoma* 69b.
80  Artscroll commentary to *Yoma* 69b.
81  Rabbi Avigdor Miller, *Toras Avigdor on Parshas Ki Sisa*, 5779.

We do not understand and Hashem does understand. "For My thoughts are not your thoughts, and your ways are not My ways, the word of Hashem."[82]

We study Torah to try to understand and live by the ways of Hashem. While much in the Torah is counterintuitive to our human minds, the Torah is written by the Creator of the Universe, and we defer to Him.

When we pray, Hashem listens. As Dovid HaMelech says, "I love Him, for Hashem hears my voice, my supplications. As He has inclined His ear to me, so in my days shall I call."[83]

## THE SEVENTEENTH BERACHAH: RETURN OF THE SHECHINAH TO TZIYON

רְצֵה ה' אֱ-לֹהֵינוּ בְּעַמְּךָ יִשְׂרָאֵל וּבִתְפִלָּתָם, וְהָשֵׁב אֶת הָעֲבוֹדָה לִדְבִיר בֵּיתֶךָ. וְאִשֵּׁי יִשְׂרָאֵל וּתְפִלָּתָם בְּאַהֲבָה תְקַבֵּל בְּרָצוֹן, וּתְהִי לְרָצוֹן תָּמִיד עֲבוֹדַת יִשְׂרָאֵל עַמֶּךָ: וְתֶחֱזֶינָה עֵינֵינוּ בְּשׁוּבְךָ לְצִיּוֹן בְּרַחֲמִים: בָּרוּךְ אַתָּה ה' הַמַּחֲזִיר שְׁכִינָתוֹ לְצִיּוֹן:

*Be favorable, Hashem, our G-d, to Your people Israel and their prayer, and restore the service to the Holy of Holies of Your Temple. Accept the fire-offerings and prayer of Israel with love and favor, and may the service of Your people Israel always be favorable to You. May our eyes behold Your return to Zion in mercy. Blessed are You, Hashem, Who restores His Presence to Zion.*

This is, to me, the most emotional and "palpable" of all the *berachos*. I see it! I feel it!

At the Kosel, those huge, impenetrable stones appear so forbidding. But, when I think about Hashem's Presence returning to dwell once again behind those stones, everything is changed. The world is changed. "The G-d of Yaakov…turns the rock into a pond of water, the flint into a flowing fountain."[84]

---

82   *Yeshayah* 55:8; haftarah for fast-day *Minchah*.
83   *Tehillim* 116.
84   Ibid. 114.

In the time of *Bayis Rishon*, the Shechinah was there, in the Beis Hamikdash. This is what we need now. "May our eyes behold Your return to Tziyon in compassion!"[85]

This is literally all we need. If this one thing would be fulfilled, we would not need anything else. When the Shechinah returns to its place, then the entire world will be rectified. "*Ki miTziyon teitzei Torah u'dvar Hashem miYerushalayim*—Then from Tziyon will go forth Torah and the word of Hashem from Yerushalayim."[86] The Shechinah needs a pure place, just a tiny opening…and Hashem will do the rest.

"Open for me an opening like the eye of a needle and I will enlarge it to be an opening through which wagons can enter."[87]

I believe that, if we keep this in mind, it will give us tremendous hope. We do not have upon our heads the responsibility to do more than we can do, but if we provide even a tiny place of purity in the world, we hope that He will do the rest and fill up the entire world with His Presence.

There is a famous song called "*Bilvavi*." Here are the words: "In my heart I shall build a Sanctuary to the splendor of His honor, and in the Sanctuary I shall place an Altar to the rays of His glory. And for an eternal flame I shall take the fire of the *Akeidas Yitzchak*.[88] And for the sacrifice I shall offer Him my soul, my one and only soul."[89]

This means we should dedicate ourselves, to the exclusion of other goals, to the goal of providing a place on earth to which Hashem's Presence can return. And, of course, that place is exactly where the Shechinah rested before, on Har Habayis. It is called "Tziyon," at the center of the world. This is the place from which the voice of Hashem emanated, from beneath the wings of the *Keruvim* that were on top of the *Aron Kodesh*.

"And when Moshe would come to the *Ohel Moed*…he would hear the voice [of Hashem] communicating with him from above the lid [of the

---

85 Language of the *berachah*.
86 *Yeshayah* 2:3.
87 *Midrash Shir Hashirim* 5:2.
88 The binding of Yitzchak.
89 Based upon a passage from *Sefer Chareidim* by Rabbi Elazar Azkari and adapted by Rabbi Yitzchak Hutner. (Rabbi Shmuel Brazil wrote the music for the well-known song.)

*Aron*].... Moshe would enter the *Mishkan*. As soon as he came into the entrance, a voice would descend from the heavens to [a point] between the *Keruvim*, and from there it would go forth and be heard by Moshe in the *Ohel Moed*."[90]

We want this to happen again. We want Hashem to speak to us. We want the voice of Hashem to direct us and guide us and command us. We want His Presence among us.

The nations of the world all covet Yerushalayim because they want precisely the opposite. They want to stop the voice of Hashem from entering the world, because if Hashem is not speaking to us—G-d forbid—then it seems (but only "seems") that they will have the freedom to do whatever they want, to live without rules and follow their selfish desires.

The nations covet Yerushalayim to try to muzzle the voice of Hashem. We can try to bring the Shechinah back.

How?

As we have discussed, we are in *galus* today because of *sinas chinam*, unwarranted hatred between Jew and Jew. We can correct this and end this exile and bring back the Shechinah by correcting our behavior, which means establishing "unwarranted love" between Jew and Jew. We are going to have to try to behave towards each other with love, even if someone doesn't seem to deserve it.

This sounds like the first *berachah*, where we ask Hashem to bring the redeemer to us, "for His Name's sake, with love." If we act with love toward our fellow Jew, even if he doesn't seem to deserve it, Hashem will act toward us with love, even though we may not deserve it. That seems the way to encourage the Shechinah to return to Tziyon, and that will be the solution to all our problems.

## THE EIGHTEENTH BERACHAH: THANK YOU!

מוֹדִים אֲנַחְנוּ לָךְ שָׁאַתָּה הוּא ה' אֱ-לֹהֵינוּ וֵא-לֹהֵי אֲבוֹתֵינוּ לְעוֹלָם וָעֶד, צוּר חַיֵּינוּ מָגֵן יִשְׁעֵנוּ אַתָּה הוּא לְדוֹר וָדוֹר, נוֹדֶה

---

[90] *Rashi* on *Shemos* 25:22.

לְךָ וּנְסַפֵּר תְּהִלָּתֶךָ עַל חַיֵּינוּ הַמְּסוּרִים בְּיָדֶךָ, וְעַל נִשְׁמוֹתֵינוּ הַפְּקוּדוֹת לָךְ, וְעַל נִסֶּיךָ שֶׁבְּכָל יוֹם עִמָּנוּ, וְעַל נִפְלְאוֹתֶיךָ וְטוֹבוֹתֶיךָ שֶׁבְּכָל עֵת, עֶרֶב וָבֹקֶר וְצָהֳרָיִם, הַטּוֹב כִּי לֹא כָלוּ רַחֲמֶיךָ, וְהַמְרַחֵם כִּי לֹא תַמּוּ חֲסָדֶיךָ, מֵעוֹלָם קִוִּינוּ לָךְ: וְעַל כֻּלָּם יִתְבָּרַךְ וְיִתְרוֹמֵם שִׁמְךָ מַלְכֵּנוּ תָּמִיד לְעוֹלָם וָעֶד: וְכֹל הַחַיִּים יוֹדוּךָ סֶּלָה וִיהַלְלוּ אֶת שִׁמְךָ בֶּאֱמֶת, הָאֵ-ל יְשׁוּעָתֵנוּ וְעֶזְרָתֵנוּ סֶלָה: בָּרוּךְ אַתָּה ה' הַטּוֹב שִׁמְךָ וּלְךָ נָאֶה לְהוֹדוֹת:

*We thank You, because You are Hashem, our G-d and the G-d of our forefathers forever; Rock of our lives. You are the Shield of our salvation from generation to generation. We will thank You and relate Your praise for our lives which are given over into Your hand, and for our souls that are entrusted to You, for Your miracles that are with us every day, and for Your wonders and favors at every moment, evening, morning, and afternoon. The Benevolent One, Your mercies never end. The Merciful One, Your kindnesses never end. Forever, our hope is in You. For all these, may Your Name be blessed and exalted, our King, continually forever and ever. Everything alive will acknowledge You forever, and sincerely praise Your Name, the Almighty Who is our salvation and help forever. Blessed are You, Hashem, "The Beneficent One" is Your Name and to You is fitting to give thanks.*

This *berachah* is so upbeat, because coming right after our prayer to bring the Shechinah back to Tziyon, we immediately say "Thank You." Perhaps we can suggest that this *berachah* is hinting to us that there will come a time, hopefully very soon, when we are going to thank Hashem for returning the Shechinah to Tziyon!

The *berachah* begins "*Modim anachnu lach.*"

"*Modim*" means "acknowledge" or "admit." What does that tell us? What does "*modim anachnu lach*" really mean? It means "I acknowledge before You, Hashem, that You are the Hashem of our Fathers for all eternity, Rock of our lives…."

To acknowledge the truth is to thank, for if you acknowledge the truth, then you are aware that you have received a great gift. If you are aware you have received a great gift, then you must be grateful for what you have received. This is proper behavior, what we call *"derech eretz,"* and *"derech eretz kadmah l'Torah*…proper behavior precedes Torah."[91]

If I see how there is nothing in my life that is not done by Hashem, if I admit to myself that I am dependent on Hashem for everything spiritual, mental, and physical, then I have to be grateful, and gratitude is the foundation of life.

If you hold a door open for someone, he should say "Thank you." Why should he expect a favor? Is there any law that good things should happen to a person? Why do we expect to live? Why do we expect to breathe? Why do we expect to walk? Why do we expect to see? Why do we expect to eat? Why do we expect to taste? Why do we expect to be healthy? Why do we expect to be happy?

Who says it is coming to us?

These are all gifts.

We begin every day with an amazing series of *berachos*:

- *Shelo asani goy*—I am not a non-Jew. There are very few Jews in the world; the probability of not being a Jew is massive. Why was I so blessed?
- *Shelo asani aved*—I am not a slave. We were once slaves in Egypt. We are slaves to the *yetzer hara*, but Hashem allows us to free ourselves. Just as we got out of Egypt, so we can get out of all forms of slavery.
- *Shelo asani ishah*—I am not a woman. When I say this, I always think how difficult it is for my wife to be married to me! Women have the formidable task of molding their husbands into *menschen*. Hashem called Chavah, *"ezer kenegdo*—the help against him."[92] A good wife helps her husband when he is behaving himself and corrects him when he needs it. This is a real partnership!

---

91  *Vayikra Rabbah* 9:3.
92  *Bereishis* 2:18.

- A woman says, *She'asani kirtzono*—Hashem made me according to His will. Thank You, Hashem, that I was created on such a high level with *binah yeseirah*.
- *Poke'ach ivrim*—Hashem gives sight to the blind. Some people cannot see. The eye is very vulnerable. Some people have insight into spiritual realms.
- *Malbish arumim*—Hashem clothes the naked. Many people do not have sufficient clothing. What about prisoners in concentration camps or Siberia, where the temperature could drop to minus fifty—they had only rags! We cannot take even the most basic necessities for granted.
- *Matir asurim*—Hashem releases the bound. There are innocent people in prison. I thank You, Hashem, that I am not in prison. Remember Reb Sholom Rubashkin who *was* in prison. In his greatness, he saw beyond the bars; he knew that his *neshamah* was not imprisoned. There have been countless Jews imprisoned unjustly during our long *galus*.
- *Zokaif kefufim*—Hashem straightens the bent. Have you ever had back pain?
- *Roka ha'aretz al hamayim*—Hashem spreads out the earth upon the waters. People get flooded. What about Hurricane Sandy? What about Houston? Dry land is a gift. So is a roof over our head.
- *She'asa li kol tzarchi*—Hashem has provided all our needs. Hashem gives us everything. It's beyond our ability to count. If we understand this, then we are satisfied in life, as it says, "*samei'ach b'chelko*—satisfied with what we have."[93]
- *Hameichin mitzadei gaver*—Hashem establishes the footsteps of man. Some people cannot walk, or their every step is painful. When you were ten years old, you ran everywhere. Can you still do that? The ability to walk is an incredible gift from *Shamayim*! Every footstep merits our gratitude to the Master of the Universe!

---

93   *Pirkei Avos* 4:1.

- *Ozeir Yisrael bigvurah*—Hashem girds Israel with strength. Can you lift something heavy? Can you exercise? Can you stand for the prayers on Yom Kippur while you are fasting? Some people have no strength. Strength to function in life is a tremendous blessing!
- *Oteir Yisrael b'sifarah*—Hashem crowns Israel with splendor. We are a glorious nation, blessed with beautiful character traits. We are descendants of kings and prophets and great rabbis who were like angels. We wear crowns of Torah. This causes the envy of the entire world, but Hashem will protect us if we are loyal to Him.
- *Hanosein laya'eif ko'ach*—Hashem gives strength to the weary. Who is not tired? Do we thank Hashem for coffee? Coffee is a blessing to those who try to overcome their own physical and mental weakness in order to serve Him. Do we thank Hashem for sleep? Do we thank Hashem that we awaken with strength for a new day?

When we go through trials in life, we should try to keep our perspective and thank Hashem even for the trials. When I look back at the difficulties I had in my life, I see they were all gifts from Hashem that helped me achieve what I needed to achieve.

I heard from Rabbi Yechezkel Shraga Weinfeld a very interesting explanation of the name Ephraim (the son of Yosef). "Ephraim" means "*Hifrani Elokim b'eretz anyi*—Hashem has made me fruitful in the land of my troubles."[94] Rabbi Weinfeld says this name indicates the following character trait: "I am living through my pains, and I see the growth through it.…The ability for a man to live through his pain and use it as an impetus for growth, is seemingly a level that is worth striving for. Ephraim embodies…the ability to grow through tribulations."

Yosef became viceroy of Egypt and saved his entire family. To this day, we bless our sons that they should be like Yosef's sons: "May Hashem make you like Ephraim and Menashe."[95]

---

94   *Bereishis* 41:52.
95   Ibid. 48:20.

When Moshiach comes, our principal focus in prayer will be to thank Hashem![96] The list of things for which we have to thank Him is literally…endless!

## THE FINAL BERACHAH: PEACE

שִׂים שָׁלוֹם טוֹבָה וּבְרָכָה חֵן וָחֶסֶד וְרַחֲמִים עָלֵינוּ וְעַל כָּל יִשְׂרָאֵל עַמֶּךָ, בָּרְכֵנוּ אָבִינוּ כֻּלָּנוּ כְּאֶחָד בְּאוֹר פָּנֶיךָ, כִּי בְאוֹר פָּנֶיךָ נָתַתָּ לָּנוּ ה' אֱ-לֹהֵינוּ, תּוֹרַת חַיִּים, וְאַהֲבַת חֶסֶד, וּצְדָקָה, וּבְרָכָה, וְרַחֲמִים, וְחַיִּים, וְשָׁלוֹם, וְטוֹב בְּעֵינֶיךָ לְבָרֵךְ אֶת עַמְּךָ יִשְׂרָאֵל בְּכָל עֵת וּבְכָל שָׁעָה בִּשְׁלוֹמֶךָ: בָּרוּךְ אַתָּה ה' הַמְבָרֵךְ אֶת עַמּוֹ יִשְׂרָאֵל בַּשָּׁלוֹם:

*Establish peace, goodness, blessing, graciousness, kindness, and compassion upon us and upon all of Your people Israel. Bless us, our Father, all of us as one, with the light of Your countenance; for with the light of Your countenance You gave us, Hashem, our G-d, the Torah of life and a love of kindness, righteousness, blessing, compassion, life, and peace. And may it be good in Your eyes to bless Your people Israel, at every season and at every moment with Your peace. Blessed are You, Hashem, Who blesses His people Israel with peace.*

Can you imagine peace and tranquility in this world?

Right now, there is war and conflict in almost every place you look. There are enemies all around. Countries are at war and individuals are at war. There is anger and danger in every direction. The world is full of insecurity, fear, and violence.

How on earth can a realistic person expect peace?

And yet the *Shemoneh Esreh* ends with a prayer for peace: "Establish abundant peace upon Your people, Israel, forever…. May it be good in Your eyes to bless Your people, Israel, at every time and every hour with Your peace…."

This is the prayer of every good-hearted person—peace!

---

96   *Mabit, Sefer Beis Elokim.*

In truth, if we would only follow Hashem's plan for us, we would see peace.

Is this not tragic? If we would do *teshuvah,* in an instant Hashem would save us! We have it in our power to bring about peace in this world.

Right now, we are threatened with the opposite of peace on a worldwide basis. The danger today is arguably as great as it has ever been in history. Our enemies are within and without.

What is the basis for my statement about the extreme degree of danger in today's world? According to what you have read until now, it will not be difficult to understand:

- The growing isolation of Israel in the world today, apparently heading toward total rejection: "The kings of the earth take their stand and the princes conspire secretly against Hashem and His anointed: 'Let us cut their cords and let us cast off their ropes from ourselves.'"[97]
- The growing worldwide moral upheaval, resembling the revolt of the generation of Noach, which caused the *Mabul,* which destroyed the entire world.
- The development of nuclear weapons, which can bring about the destruction of the entire world, G-d forbid, and growing world chaos, which gives amoral people access to almost unlimited destructive power. "For behold, the day is coming, burning like an oven, when all the wicked people will be like straw...."[98]

The *Rambam* says that in the time of Moshiach, the righteous will be at peace to study Torah without interruption and anguish. As we said above,

> *The Sages and Prophets did not yearn for the Messianic era in order to have dominion over the entire world to rule over the gentiles, to be exalted by the nations, or to eat, drink, and celebrate. Rather [they desired] to be free [to involve themselves] in Torah and wisdom without any pressures or disturbances, so that they would merit the world to come....*

---

97  *Tehillim* 2.
98  *Malachi* 3:19.

> *In that era...the occupation of the entire world will be solely to know Hashem...as [the Navi][99] states: "The world will be filled with the knowledge of Hashem as the waters cover the ocean bed."[100]*

Every day, when we say the *Shemoneh Esreh*, we pray for peace. It would be so easy to attain if we would but listen to Hashem's words.

> *Listen, My Nation and I will attest to you, O Israel, if you would but listen to Me! There shall be no strange god within you, nor shall you bow before an alien god. I am Hashem, your Hashem, Who elevated you from the land of Egypt. Open wide your mouth and I will fill it. But My people did not heed My voice and Israel did not desire Me. So I let them follow their heart's fantasies; I let them follow their own counsels. If only My people would heed Me, if Israel would walk in My ways, in an instant I would subdue their foes and turn My hand against their enemies![101]*

It's right there, my friends. We have the key to peace in our hands. We have only to put the key in the lock, turn it, and open the door!

> *For this commandment that I command you today – it is not hidden from you and it is not distant. It is not in heaven, [for you] to say, 'Who can ascend to the heaven for us and take it for us, so that we can listen to it and perform it?' Nor is it across the sea, [for you] to say, 'Who can cross to the other side of the sea for us and take it for us, so that we can listen to it and perform it?' Rather the matter is very near to you, in your mouth and in your heart, to perform it.[102]*

Peace is so close. Torah is so close. We have only to reach out for it!

---

99   *Yeshayah* 11:9.
100  *Rambam, Hilchos Melachim* 12:4–5.
101  *Tehillim* 81.
102  *Devarim* 30:11ff.

*Chapter 8*

# ISOLATION AND REDEMPTION

Bilaam said of B'nei Yisrael, *"Am levadad yishkon*—Behold, it is a nation that will dwell in solitude and not be reckoned among the nations."[1] He was an evil prophet, but he was a prophet, and he declared the truth.

We are a nation apart.

We were not meant to be a part of any nation, and yet we have contracted a sickness in which we desperately try to ally ourselves with our enemies, as if we need them in order for us to feel that we can "belong" to the nations of the world.

This sickness is potentially fatal. There is only one place we belong, and that is ensconced in our unique and direct relationship with the King of the Universe.

Only through this unique relationship can we survive. All history has taught us this. What we call "anti-Semitism" is a message from our Father in Heaven, who pushes us away from this poisonous relationship with the empty nations who hate us.

It is all coming to an end now. Soon we will have been rejected by every nation and every individual among the nations. The entire world is rejecting Israel and each individual Jew. We are outcasts. Hashem is sending this upon us to force us to wake up.

---

1 *Bamidbar* 23:9.

The rabbis of the Talmud discuss how Klal Yisrael will repent before Moshiach comes, and this is what they say: "Rabbi Yehoshua said to [Rabbi Eliezer], 'If they do not repent, they will not be redeemed?!' [Yes, they will repent, but how will it come about?]

"[Hashem] will appoint a king over them whose decrees will be as harsh as [those of] Haman, and the Jewish People will repent, and in this way [Hashem] will bring them back to the right [path]."[2]

We cannot dismiss this, because this is Torah.

Anti-Semitism is bitter medicine, but it is apparently what we require to cure our sickness.

The events of Biblical Egypt occurred in order to separate us from the Egyptians. Their hatred pushed us away from them. So too today, the violent hatred in today's world is apparently necessary because we are so attracted to these nations that we do not know how to extricate ourselves.

Rabbi Yechiel Yitzchok Perr, Rosh Yeshiva of the Yeshiva of Far Rockaway, said in February 2019, "The ejection from America has begun."

The Jews have been ejected from many lands. Rabbi Chaim Volozhin is quoted as having said that the "last stop" for the Jews before Moshiach would be America, and now we are being ejected from America.[3] The next stop is the final redemption.

The Modern Age is founded upon "technology." Technology has become the pride of world culture and is considered the path to the "new paradise." It has also become the addiction of world culture. It is very hard to believe that the downfall of world culture will not be accompanied by the downfall of its idol.

Technology is about to disintegrate along with the culture that idolizes it.

We have to prepare for this. We have to understand that we are completely alone in the world. There is nothing to save us besides the King

---

2   *Sanhedrin* 97b.
3   *Mishnas R' Aron, chelek* 4 (speeches of Rabbi Aharon Kotler).

of the Universe. All our toys will soon be taken away, and nothing will remain but reality.

This is the place to repeat the words of the late Rabbi Shimshon Pincus:

> We live in a "modern" world, but with all its technological advances…the results are shockingly poor. Everything is put to use for the bad. The world was a more beautiful place without modern cameras and their streams of indecent images that now flood the world. And so it is with technology's other products. There is no modern invention that did not do harm to the world, without exception.[4]

This was written decades ago, before the situation became much worse.

Rabbi Yosef Shalom Elyashiv said regarding the internet, "Since Creation, the evil inclination never had such a powerful, destructive tool."[5]

Rabbi Chaim Yisroel Belsky quotes the *pasuk*, "And I have created a weapon to wreak destruction,"[6] as referring to the internet.[7]

Mankind has gone far toward destroying the earth and heavens. So far, we have not reached much beyond our own solar system, but we leave a path of pollution and destruction everywhere we go. Ever since we were expelled from Gan Eden for rebelling against Hashem's laws, we have proceeded to destroy the earth progressively more and more, and in the last two centuries, since the "technological revolution," that destruction has speeded up, so that, today, it is out of control. It is taking over from us and has become our master, so that "cars driving people" is not an exaggeration.

Indeed, those who cling to the "god" of technology are becoming robots: mindless and heartless. Today, people walk down the street with metal clips in their ears, reminiscent of the Biblical slave who chooses to remain attached to his master and is bound by Torah law to pierce

---

4   *Nefesh Shimshon*, p. 273.
5   Artscroll biography, p. 401.
6   *Yeshayah* 54:16.
7   *Sefer Einei Yisrael*, p. 154.

his ear with a metal awl. People stare with empty eyes at electronic screens and walk across the intersection oblivious to the car that is bearing down on them. This world of the living dead is the "paradise" we have created.

Let us remember how life on this earth began. Hashem created a perfect world, where everything coexisted in harmony. There was no death, sickness, or pain. There was nothing missing, spiritually or physically. All food was supplied with no lack of anything, and nothing had to be killed so anyone could live. Nothing was wasted.

When I say "nothing was wasted," there was no litter. There was no plastic. There were no garbage dumps because there was no garbage. Everything that was consumed was used completely. When you ate fruit from the tree, nothing was killed, and the tree was "happy" because it was created so you could pick its fruit. It was like a mother nursing her child; the mother is happy, and the child is happy. All is good and nothing is wasted or destroyed.

When mankind was expelled from Gan Eden, immediately there was trouble. Kayin killed Hevel out of jealousy. When it came time to eat meat, animals had to be killed. When man put on shoes, animals had to be killed for their hides. Meat was permitted so that man could survive, but in order for a man to eat, another creature was killed.

Eventually we come to the modern age where we are buried in our own garbage, and we have poured concrete over the earth in our restless obsession with building and travel. Since we were expelled from Gan Eden, we are constantly unhappy. We run around the world desperately looking for a paradise which we cannot find.

Was there "technology" in Gan Eden?

For what? The world was perfect.

But now that man has come to believe there is no G-d in the world, he tries to create his own version of Gan Eden, his own version of perfection, his own idea of paradise. From his seething brain, which thinks only about physical needs, he comes up with countless inventions, and each one makes the world worse. We now have weapons that can kill people around the world with pinpoint accuracy or reduce the entire planet to a radioactive junk pile, killing and maiming the entire human race and destroying the beautiful and perfect world that Hashem created for us.

As mentioned above, each blade of grass has its own angel that tells it, "Grow! Grow!" and watches out for it. What do you think the grass feels when the bulldozer is destroying the field, with all the trees and plants and animals that Hashem created? It is screaming to its angel and saying, "Save me! Save me!" The field and the plants and the animals are screaming to Hashem to save them from the bulldozer, the shopping center, the highway, the skyscraper, the factory, the heavy boots of foolish men who are polluting the world—even the oceans!—with garbage.

Now you know why, when Moshiach comes and saves the world from mankind's destruction, "the heavens will be glad and the earth will rejoice and say among the nations, 'Hashem has reigned.' The sea and its fullness will roar, the field and everything in it will exult. The trees of the forest will sing with joy before Hashem, for He will have arrived to judge the earth...."[8]

The earth itself and all of Hashem's creations are praying for Moshiach to come to save them from the ravages of depraved mankind.

Mankind is reversing the order of Creation that was instituted by the Master of the World. What He created, we are trying to reverse. Soon we will reach the point where it all began, "when the earth was astonishingly empty, with darkness upon the surface of the deep...."[9]

We are returning the world to a state of utter chaos.

> In the six-hundredth year of the sixth millennium [which corresponds to the year 1840] the supernal gates of wisdom will be opened. This will prepare the world for the seventh millennium like a person prepares himself on Friday for Shabbos, as the sun begins to wane. So it will be here. There is a hint about this in the following pasuk:[10] "In the six-hundredth

---

8 Tehillim 98; Hodu.
9 Bereishis 1:1.
10 Ibid. 7:11.

> *year of Noach's life…all the fountains of the great deep were broken up, and the windows of heaven were opened."*[11]

The trouble is that mankind has corrupted this eruption from the heights and from the depths as we corrupted life inside Gan Eden, and we have turned it all to materialism instead of spiritual wisdom, so that the *Mabul* that has come upon the earth is destruction, like the *Mabul* in the days of Noach.

Indeed, the fountains of the deep and the apertures in the firmament are opening. Deep and dangerous waters are flooding the world. The storm is coming and the sky is darkening. I am reminded of the famous remark of Viscount Edward Grey in 1914, at the outbreak of World War I: "The lamps are going out all over Europe. We shall not see them lit again in our lifetime."

This time, the lamps are going out all over the world, and we shall not see them lit again until a new light shines upon the world, as we say, "May You shine a new light on Tziyon and may we all speedily merit its light!"[12]

I believe that we can say that the world after the coming upheaval will be totally different from the world of today. The corruption that has surrounded us since we were expelled from *Gan Eden* will destroy itself and we will return to a pure world…provided that we survive the coming upheaval.

It is not just the world of Yishmael and Edom—Islam and the Church of Rome—that will disappear, but Oriental culture as well, regarding which the late Rabbi Yisroel Belsky said:

> *Our rabbis tell us that there is one place in the world outside the Land of Israel where idol worship was exceedingly strong. That is somewhere in the Far East. The late Rabbi Yitzchok Hutner used to explain that the reason we see so much idol worship emanating from the Far East is sourced in the [following] words of the Torah: "To the children of Avraham's*

---

11  Zohar 1:117a.
12  *Shacharis.*

> *concubines Avraham gave gifts, and he sent them away from Yitzchak his son, while he was still alive, eastward to the land of the East."* Rashi...writes that the gifts that Avraham gave to the children of his concubines were the *"sheim tumah—the names of impurity."* In other words, Avraham gave them the pseudo-spiritual practices rooted in the *"sitra achara—the dimension of impurity."* This *"storehouse"* of impure wisdom was sent to the Far East, as suggested by the repetition of the words *"kedmah...kedem"* (in the Biblical verse just quoted). Apparently, Avraham tried to get rid of all this impurity by sending it far out, but he was not completely successful.[13]

We can see that the entire world is filled with impurity and idolatry.

Unbridled and uncontrolled technology embodies the final spurt and energy of the worldwide rebellion against Hashem. I believe that technology may be the most powerful example of idolatry in history, because it is universal, finding its way into almost every home on earth, where it is accepted as being essential to life. Even religious Jewish homes are open to this poison, and world commerce is based completely on technology. Without computers and internet, no aspect of the modern world would function.

And so, when it crashes, world civilization will crash with it.

Based on everything we have seen up to now, it appears that we have reached the end, and we are on the brink of the ultimate redemption.

It is all too much to contemplate. One cannot fathom the depth of what is ahead, and one cannot fathom the height of what is coming after that. It is easy to be afraid of the War of Gog and Magog. It is easy to be afraid of what will happen to us in this catastrophe of all catastrophes. One cannot contemplate it.

But one has no choice. We are alive now in this beleaguered world, and the fate of the world is beyond our ability to control. *"Rabos*

---

13   *Rav Belsky on Alternative Medicine* (Judaica Press, 2017), pp. 15–16.

*machashavos b'lev ish*—Many thoughts are in the heart of man, but the counsel of Hashem, only it will prevail."[14]

And so, we frail mortals stand here, at the edge of doom, at the brink of the precipice, and we imagine what will be. We do not know. And we are afraid.

Have you ever stood at the edge of the Grand Canyon? Many visitors have died there. People fool around at the edge of the cliff. They do not take it seriously…and then they lose their footing. The next ledge may be a mile below them.

In our days, the danger is great. The drop has no end. There is nothing below us. And we are fooling around.

One should be afraid, yet we are not supposed to be afraid.

Dovid HaMelech says, "Hashem is with me; I have no fear,"[15] and this is how we are supposed to be. Ah, but this takes work. This takes an effort to achieve a sense of reality, to try to understand what is really happening in the world. I doubt that Moshe was afraid of the collapse of Egypt, but he was Moshe Rabbeinu!

Can we reach the level at which we are so close to Hashem that, indeed, we can walk into the future unafraid? Certainly, it is better to be unafraid. Fear paralyzes a person, so it is better for us if we are not afraid. It is not good to go into the coming period unable to act, because, in a situation of danger, it is not good to be paralyzed.

But how does one achieve it?

I have been working on this my entire life because I have been afraid, literally since as long as I can remember. I want to tell you one thing about being afraid: it does something for you. If you try to deal with it honestly, then I believe it makes you a religious person. If you are afraid and you are able to admit it (which is not easy), then you eventually discover that you need Hashem. You have to hang on to Hashem if you are afraid, because you learn that there is nothing else to hang on to.

---

14  *Mishlei* 19:21.
15  *Tehillim* 118.

And so, I have to thank fear! Yes, I have to thank fear itself, and I have to thank Hashem for the fear and for enabling me to admit that I was afraid. But you have to learn how fear can help you.

If we understand our own helplessness, our weakness, our inability to control the world, then perhaps we will return in *teshuvah*, repentance, to the Master of the Universe, fall upon our face, and beg Him to save us. "But we bend our knees, bow and acknowledge our thanks before the King Who reigns over kings, the Holy One, blessed be He. He stretches out the heavens and establishes earth's foundation. The seat of His homage is in the heavens above and His powerful Presence is in the loftiest heights."[16]

> *What can we say before You, Hashem, our G-d and the G-d of our fathers? Are not all the heroes like nothing before You, the famous as if they never existed, the wise as if devoid of wisdom and the perceptive as if devoid of intelligence? For most of their deeds are desolate and the days of their lives are empty before You. The preeminence of man over beast is nonexistent, for all is vain.*[17]

Dovid HaMelech was totally honest. Who else could have said, "I am a worm and not a man, scorn of humanity, despised of nations."[18] Do you think he didn't mean it? Of course he meant it! What courage!

But Dovid HaMelech is also the mightiest hero, the man who stepped out alone to face Goliyas! Dovid is the one who said, "It is You who will light my lamp. Hashem, my G-d, will illuminate my darkness. For with You I smash a troop, and with my G-d I leap a wall! The G-d! His way is perfect. The promise of Hashem is flawless. He is a shield for all who take refuge in Him."[19]

They go together—the weakness and the total dependence upon Hashem, the fear and the triumph!

---

16  *Aleinu.*
17  *Shacharis.*
18  *Tehillim* 22.
19  Ibid. 18.

And so, we stand before the future.

When Moshe Rabbeinu ascended Har Sinai to meet Hashem, he first had to penetrate a cloud of darkness, as it says, "Behold, I come to you in the thickness of the cloud…"[20] We have to take this seriously. Moshe had to go through the deepest darkness to reach Hashem.

Please contemplate the following words. I imagine that you have never seen this before. I certainly had not.

> *If we would have had the [merit] of seeing into the Mishkan, we might have been surprised to see how dark it was inside. There were no windows. A small amount of light may have come in around the sides and the bottom of the thick curtain at the entrance. For a short time, there also would have been some light from the glow of the coals on the Altar of Incense. And of course, there was the glorious Menorah whose beautiful and pure light would dispel all darkness while it was lit.*
>
> *But, nevertheless, the Mishkan was…dark…. The Creator dwells in darkness. His Presence is hidden…. His thoughts, and the reasons for that which He brings upon man, are also hidden. Klal Yisrael, the Children of Israel, wait patiently, knowing the Creator is hidden and that therefore His plan is hidden. And we are thereby elevated by the test of our not knowing when….*[21]

And so, we stand here today, looking out into the future—if we have the courage to do so—and we see darkness and terror ahead of us and around us. We imagine unbearable pain and chaos beyond comprehension. The words of the *tochechah* come to mind: "You will go mad from the sight of your eyes…."[22]

---

20   *Shemos* 19:9.

21   Rabbi Yechiel Yitzchok Perr, Rosh Yeshiva, Yeshiva of Far Rockaway, *Shabbos Parashas Terumah* 5779 (February 2019).

22   *Devarim* 28:34.

Many people today are nervous, tense, worried by the future and all the things that could and might go wrong, all the pressures of life, and all the worries that could possibly be.

And there is plenty to worry about.

Why should we feel such stress and have no ability to deal with it? Should we not be calm and full of confidence in Hashem's protection? Does Dovid HaMelech not say, "Whoever sits in the refuge of the Most High, he shall dwell in the shadow of the Almighty. I will say of Hashem, 'He is my refuge and my fortress. My Hashem, I will trust in Him,' that He will deliver you from the ensnaring trap and from devastating pestilence. With His pinion He will cover you and beneath His wings you will be protected...."[23]

Why do we not feel calm and protected?

That in itself is a source of anxiety.

Our ideal is the following: "You shall be wholehearted with Hashem,"[24] which *Rashi* understands to mean: "Look ahead to Him and do not delve into the future. But rather, whatever comes upon you, accept with wholeheartedness and then you will be with Him and of His portion."

> *Perhaps you shall say in your heart, "These nations are more numerous than I. How will I be able to drive them out?" Do not fear them! You shall remember what Hashem your G-d did to Pharaoh and to all of Egypt. The great tests that your eyes saw and the signs, the wonders, the strong hand and the outstretched arm with which Hashem your G-d took you out, so shall Hashem your G-d do to all the peoples before whom you fear...*[25]
>
> *It will be when all these things come upon you—the blessing and the curse that I have presented before you—then you will take it to your heart among all the nations where Hashem your G-d has dispersed you, and you will return unto Hashem,*

---

23   *Tehillim* 91.
24   *Devarim* 18:13.
25   Ibid., 7:17–19.

> *your G-d, and listen to His voice, according to everything that I command you today, you and your children, with all your heart and all your soul. Then Hashem, your G-d, will bring back your captivity and have mercy upon you, and He will gather you in from all the peoples to which Hashem, your G-d, has scattered you. If your dispersal will be at the ends of heaven, from there Hashem, your G-d, will gather you in and from there He will take you. Hashem, your G-d, will bring you to the land that your forefathers possessed, and you shall possess it. He will do good to you and make you more numerous than your forefathers. Hashem, your G-d, will circumcise your heart, and the heart of your offspring, to love Hashem, your G-d, with all your heart and with all your soul, that you may live.[26]*

Being "wholehearted with Hashem" is not a frill. Unless one has this connection with Hashem, one will not be able to steady himself when the whirlwind comes. We must find an anchor in the storm and not fall apart. We must hold on to the rope. "Be strong and courageous, do not be afraid and do not be broken before them, for Hashem, your G-d, it is He Who goes before you. He will not release you, nor will He forsake you."[27]

How do we get there?

When our teacher, Moshe Rabbeinu, first came to Egypt to liberate B'nei Yisrael from slavery, they were unable to listen to him. Why? Because they were panicked. They were trembling from mental and physical enslavement, subjected to control by outside forces that were at every moment trying to tear them away from their connection with the Ruler of the Universe, Who was calling to them through Moshe. But they could not hear Moshe because they were so panicked.

---

26 Ibid., 30:1–6.
27 Ibid., 31:6.

It says in the Torah, "Moshe spoke…to B'nei Yisrael, but they did not heed Moshe because of shortness of breath and hard work."[28]

Moshe, the greatest teacher in Israel and the greatest person who ever lived, was speaking to our ancestors and they did not hear him.

Why? The Torah calls it "shortness of breath and hard work."

One can suffer from physical symptoms of panic that prevent one from dealing with one's situation and understanding what is going on. In the midst of deep *galus,* our souls are under such stress that words of Torah are not reaching us, and we do not know where to find Hashem, just as in the days of the Egyptian exile.

Many of us never stop to breathe. This may sound foolish, but it is true. From childhood we race through life, never stopping for breath.

Hashem wants us to remember Torah constantly.

> *Let these matters that I command you today be upon your heart. Teach them thoroughly to your children and speak of them while you sit in your home, while you walk on the way, when you retire and you arise. Bind them as a sign upon your arm and let them be tefillin between your eyes. And write them on the doorposts of your house and upon your gates.*[29]

There is virtually no moment, except while we are sleeping, when we are not supposed to keep Torah in front of us. It should be our constant occupation. "This book of the Torah shall not depart from your mouth, rather you should contemplate it day and night in order that you observe to do according to all that is written in it, for then you will make your way successful and you will act wisely."[30]

We are commanded to look at the tzitzis "so that you may see it and remember all the commandments of Hashem and perform them, and not explore after your heart and after your eyes after which you stray."[31]

But what if we are under so much stress that we are unable to focus?

---

28  *Shemos* 6:9.
29  *Devarim* 6:6.
30  *Yehoshua* 1:8.
31  *Bamidbar* 15:39.

Learning Torah and performing mitzvos cures everything, but we are blocked from proper performance of the mitzvos and learning Torah by pressures emanating from the culture in which we are living. Torah concepts are extremely difficult to acquire if one is steeped in the outside culture. Personally, I had to learn to slow myself down physically by remembering to breathe. I had to learn to breathe.

I found that when I remembered to breathe,

- I was able to concentrate better when I said a *berachah*,
- I was able to concentrate better when learning Torah,
- I was able to control my emotions better,
- I was able to calm anger and feelings of hatred,
- I was able to control obsession with food,
- I was able to overcome fear.

When I remembered to breathe, my body was controlling me less and I was controlling my body more. This exercise had an effect on my entire system.

The *Rambam* writes about anger that it is "a terrible trait, and a person must distance himself until the extreme and teach himself not to become angry even when called for."[32]

"Even when called for!" This is indeed a *madreigah*!

How does one fulfill this prescription? How does one learn to forgive another Jew? How does one control anger? I find this almost impossible to fulfill. But we are asking Hashem to make us this way, to do the "impossible" with us, just as He has done with every Jew and the entire Jewish nation up to now throughout history.

How does one control anger? I have found that stopping to take a breath enables me to exert some control over negative emotions like anger.

Torah study expands your brain beyond what you believed possible.

You are sure that you cannot understand something in the Gemara. It is "impossible" to understand. Torah is, after all, Hashem's "way of thinking," which is, by definition, infinitely beyond us. But then you

---

32   *Hilchos Deos* 2:4.

work to understand, and Hashem changes the nature of your intellect so that it "gets bigger," and you can begin to understand something you thought was totally beyond you.

How do we deal with the "impossible" challenges of modern life?

We need strategies.

The desires of the physical body represent a huge stumbling block for us. All sin began in Gan Eden when Chavah wanted to taste a fruit that was forbidden to her. She gave in, and that is where all the troubles and tragedies of history started.

Have you ever studied *Tefillah Zakah*, which we say before *Kol Nidrei* on Yom Kippur? It is the most graphic prayer I have ever seen. I am shocked every year when I read this courageous prayer by an exalted rabbi who was not afraid to describe the tremendous power of physical obsession. As the Torah tells us, at the beginning of history, in the days of Noach, "Hashem saw that the wickedness of man was great upon the earth, and that every product of the thoughts of his heart was but evil always."[33] This is mankind and this is how our heart becomes focused on our bodily cravings and emotions and pulls us with tremendous force toward a lifestyle that is not based on following the Torah of our Creator.

It all began with a desire to eat a certain food!

Following the desires of the body is what leads us downward toward the depths of destruction. Today our entire world is close to extinction because we are focused on satisfying the cravings and desires of our physical beings.

I personally experienced this. I realized that I was becoming very tired from eating. The more I ate, the more tired I was becoming, and I felt I needed to be alert and productive. I started to eat less so that I could think more clearly. It was not a diet; it was an effort to accomplish as much as possible. I became aware that I am no longer a teenager and my time is limited. Not only that, but when I think about the state of the world, I realize it is urgent to act before it is too late. I decided to eat less

---

33   *Bereishis* 6:5.

in order to accomplish more. I don't do this as much as I should, but I am having some success, and it works, because digestion takes physical energy, and one can become tired from eating.

Once we become aware of how focused we are on satisfying the desires of the body, we can try to wean ourselves from our obsession and focus on how we can improve our ways of serving Hashem, asking him to save us as the world turns upside down.

When I became upset with the present world scene, I started to think of the past as if it were better than today. I brought back pleasant memories of years gone by, of people like my parents who are no longer here and who represented a lifestyle that is very different from today's lifestyle, even though we are talking about only a span of a few years. But Shlomo HaMelech told us, "Do not say, 'How was it that former times were better than these?' for that is not a question prompted by wisdom."[34] And then I realized that my pleasant memories of the past were an illusion, because when I was younger, I had not yet found Hashem. The fact is that every moment was confused, and I felt totally helpless without Hashem.

The world is changing fast. As we have discussed, much of it is now in the hands of madmen, and these madmen are armed with weapons that can wipe out all life and make the world unbearable for those who survive. These madmen know how to use these weapons. They also do not care about the life of the world; they care about their own lives and the things they personally desire.

As the world becomes more clearly insane, the idea grows on us that we need to go beyond our own experience to find our anchor in the chaos, the Rock to which we will cling. Indeed, Moshe Rabbeinu says: "The Rock: perfect is His work, for all His paths are justice, a Hashem of faith without iniquity, righteous and fair is He. Corruption is not His; the blemish is His children's, a perverse and twisted generation...."[35]

I thought I had seen a good world in the past, but then I realized that I had no experience of the world the way it is supposed to be. For that,

---

34  *Koheles* 7:10.
35  *Devarim* 32:4–5.

one must return to Gan Eden, or the days when the Beis Hamikdash stood in the Holy City of Yerushalayim, and no one alive today has seen those things.

> *How majestic was the Kohen Gadol as he left the Kodesh Hakodashim in peace, without injury.... Like the heavenly canopy stretched out over those who dwell above was the appearance of the Kohen Gadol...Like lightning bolts emanating from the radiance of the chayos...Like the fringes attached to the four corners.... Like the image of the rainbow amid the cloud...Like a rose placed amid a precious garden...Like a crown placed on a king's forehead...Like the morning star on the eastern border was the appearance of the Kohen Gadol.... Fortunate is the eye that saw all these....[36]*

There is no halfway. Either the world must be the way Hashem created it to be, or it will be nothing. That is where we are now. Once maybe we could pretend that we could get away with deviating from the path of Torah, but no longer. It is totally clear in our era that only Torah will save us, as we see the world hurtling towards destruction. There will be no halfway.

In the beginning, the world was "astonishingly empty, with darkness upon the surface of the deep."[37] That is how the world began and that is where we are now.

This is the end. It is also the beginning.

We have to know that the world will be perfect again.

Hashem is over all. "*Rabos machashavos b'lev ish*—Many thoughts are in man's heart, but only the will of Hashem will prevail."[38] Mankind's foolish schemes are at an end.

I hope we will have the strength to focus on Hashem when the explosion comes, because we will need incredible strength and we will

---

36   *Mussaf* of Yom Kippur.
37   *Bereishis* 1:2.
38   *Mishlei* 19:21.

have to be prepared as best we can. If we are taken by surprise, we will not make it.

But the new world…ah, the new world. I do not pretend to know what it will be, except what one can glean from the prophets, but…it will be a world of perfection, a world of peace, filled with Torah. No longer will we have to eat our bread by the sweat of our brow.

> *A staff will emerge from the stump of Yishai and a shoot will sprout from his roots. The spirit of Hashem will rest upon him, a spirit of wisdom and understanding, a spirit of counsel and strength, a spirit of knowledge and fear of Hashem. He will…not need to judge by what his eyes see nor decide by what his ears hear. He will judge the destitute with righteousness and decide with fairness for the humble of the earth. He will strike [the wicked]…with the rod of his mouth and with the breath of his lips he will slay the wicked. Righteousness will be the girdle around his loins, and faith will be the girdle around his waist.*
>
> *The wolf will live with the sheep and the leopard will lie down with the kid…They will neither injure nor destroy in all of My sacred mountain, for the earth will be filled with knowledge of G-d as water covering the seabed. It shall be on that day that the descendant of Yishai who stands as a banner for the peoples, nations will seek him, and his resting place will be glorious. It shall be on that day that the Lord will once again show His hand, to acquire the remnant of His people who will have remained…He will raise a banner for the nations and assemble the castaways of Israel, and He will gather in the dispersed ones of Judah from the four corners of the earth.*[39]

May Hashem, Who has guided us through history, guide us through the coming years so that we reach this moment in peace and safety. We have to do everything possible to merit redemption, but we are deep in

---

39   *Yeshayah* 11:1ff.

exile, and, in the end, it is only "*l'ma'an Shemo b'ahavah*…for the sake of His Name, with love,"[40] that Hashem will send the redeemer, just the way He sent a redeemer to our ancestors in ancient Egypt.

The Prophet says:

> The Word of Hashem…. "I scattered [the House of Israel] among the nations and they were dispersed among the lands. According to their ways and their doings did I judge them, and they came to the nations…and they desecrated My holy Name when it was said of them, 'These are Hashem's people, but they departed His land.' But I pitied My holy Name that the House of Israel desecrated among the nations to which they came.
>
> "Therefore, say to the House of Israel…. Thus says my Lord, Hashem: Not for your sake do I act, O House of Israel, but for My Holy Name that you have desecrated among the nations to which you came. And I will sanctify My great name that was desecrated among the nations, that you desecrated among them. Then the nations shall know that I am Hashem—the words of My Lord, Hashem—when I become sanctified through you in their sight.
>
> "And I shall take you from the nations and gather you in from all the countries, and I shall bring you to your land, and I shall sprinkle pure water upon you, that you be cleansed. From all your contamination and from all your filth I will cleanse you, and I shall give you a new heart and a new spirit shall I put within you. I shall remove the heart of stone from your flesh and give you a heart of flesh. And My spirit shall I put within you, and I shall cause you to go by My decrees and guard My laws and perform them, and you shall dwell in the land that I gave your fathers, and you shall be to Me a people, and I shall be your G-d.

---

40   First *berachah* of *Shemoneh Esreh*.

"And I shall save you from all your contaminations and I shall summon the grain and increase it, and I shall not place famine upon you, and I shall increase the fruit of the tree and the produce of the field so that you no longer accept the shame of hunger among the nations. Then you will remember your evil ways and your doings that were not good, and you shall loathe yourselves in your own sight because of your sins and your abominations. Not for your sake do I act—the word of My Lord, Hashem—let it be known to you. Be ashamed and be humiliated because of your ways, O House of Israel."

Thus says my Lord Hashem: "On the day when I cleanse you from all your sins, and cause the cities to be inhabited and the ruins to be rebuilt and the desolated land to be tilled instead of being desolate in the eyes of every passerby, then they shall say, 'This very land that was desolate has become a Garden of Eden and the cities that were destroyed and were desolate and ruined shall be fortified…inhabited!' And the nations that will remain around you will know that I am Hashem, I will have rebuilt the ruins, replanted the wasteland. I, Hashem, have spoken and acted."[41]

> Remember the exhausted [nation] that won [Your favor], and return her to Your soil.[42]
>
> Please be revealed, and spread upon me, my Beloved, the shelter of Your peace. Illuminate the world with Your glory that we may rejoice and be glad with You. Hasten, show love, for the time has come, and show us grace as in days of old.[43]

---

41 *Yechezkel* 36:16–36.
42 *Tefillah* before Yom Tov *Mussaf*.
43 *Yedid Nefesh*.

# EPILOGUE

Let us try to sum up.

Every day, we mention *yetzias Mitzrayim*.

Every Friday night, we make *Kiddush* "*zeicher l'yetzias Mitzrayim*—in remembrance of the Exodus from Egypt."

Why does the Torah insist on remembering this ancient event?

I believe that we can say the Torah is looking ahead and telling us that we are going to experience another *yetzias Mitzrayim* at the end of history.

The Torah wants us to know that no matter what, just the way our ancestors escaped from the "inescapable" prison of ancient Egypt, so we too, at the end of history, will be able to escape from our "inescapable" prison and march once again to a new "Har Sinai," where we will meet the Master of the Universe. He will once again give us His Torah, and then we will once again have a Beis Hamikdash in Yerushalayim.

But this time it will never be taken away.

"He will let us hear, in His compassion, for a second time in the presence of all the living…'to be a G-d to you, I am Hashem, your G-d.'"[1]

My friends, Hashem is going to send us a redeemer just the way He sent a redeemer to our ancestors in Egypt.

"Several times I heard from the holy Chofetz Chaim, that we can learn about the end of our exile from what happened at the end of our exile in Egypt, as it says,[2] 'As in the days of your leaving Egypt, I will show wonders [in the final redemption].'"[3]

---

1    *Kedushah* of Shabbos *Mussaf*.
2    *Michah* 7:15.
3    Rabbi Elchonon Wasserman, in a letter (*Meir Einei Yisrael* 2, p. 460), seen in *Redemption Unfolding*, p. 78.

The story of *yetzias Mitzrayim* is our guarantee that we will be able to escape from this *galus*.

"Whoever sits in the refuge of the most High, he shall dwell in the shadow of the Almighty.... You shall not be afraid of the terror of night nor of the arrow that flies by day, nor the pestilence that walks in gloom, nor the destroyer who lays waste at noon.... For he has yearned for Me and I will deliver him. I will elevate him because he knows My Name. He will call upon Me and I will answer him. I am with him in distress. I will release him and I will honor him. With long life I will satisfy him and I will show him My salvation...."[4]

Today we are prisoners in a global prison, which resembles the prison of ancient Egypt.

- Every person is subject to increasing control by "Big Brother." In China, a half-billion security cameras identify and track every individual. This trend is spreading throughout the world.
- Commerce is controlled by giant corporations beyond anyone's ability to scrutinize. Gone is the corner store whose owner was your friend, whose products were made by people you knew. Now goods are manufactured on the other side of the globe, ordered online, and delivered by drone. What was available yesterday is not available today. Where did it go?
- A faceless government decrees what our yeshivos should teach, and faceless inspectors take over the administration.
- Policemen wear cameras; even they are being watched.
- People wear speakers in their ears and electronic glasses; they hear what they are programmed to hear and see what they are programmed to see.
- Pedestrians attached to cell phones communicate by pressing buttons as they bump into light poles or walk in front of cars.
- Masses of people march to the drumbeat of a media face who tells them what is going on in the world, whom they should hate, and whom they should cheer.

---

4   *Tehillim* 91.

The technological "Garden of Eden" has become a black hole, a whirlpool sucking us downward into oblivion.

But suddenly *"k'heref ayin*—in the blink of an eye,"[5] the prison door will open. Just when we think we will never escape, Hashem will rescue us.

"Pharaoh sent and summoned Yosef, and they rushed him from the dungeon."[6] Yehudah and his brothers were at the very end, despairing, hopeless. The madman in front of them was threatening an eternal end to the light brought into the world by their fathers Avraham, Yitzchak, and Yaakov.

Blackness was closing in. And then, out of the darkness came a voice: "Ani Yosef…I am Yosef."[7]

> *Dovid…was the mightiest of kings, the most pious of the pious, wisest among the wise, humble among the modest, and the most glorious of poets who sang praise before G-d. Notwithstanding all this, no one suffered as much anguish in his life as Dovid…which did not leave him until his very last day, when his son Shlomo succeeded him…. Indeed, Dovid's secret was concealed from his father and mother, from [his brothers and] all the people who lived in his time, and even from Shmuel HaNavi, who did not recognize [his] abilities even after he first saw him, until Hashem told him, "Rise! Anoint him, for he is the one!"*[8]

"*Uva l'Tziyon go'el*—a redeemer will come to Tziyon and to those who repent from willful sin—the word of Hashem."[9] And so, we grasp the rope that Hashem has lowered into this world, the umbilical cord that connects us to *Shamayim*. No matter how the rope shakes and the earth

---

5  *Pesikta Zutra* on *Esther* 4:17.
6  *Bereishis* 41:14.
7  Ibid., 45:3.
8  *Book of Our Heritage*, chapter entitled "Rus and Dovid."
9  *Yeshayah* 59:20.

trembles, no matter how dark the world becomes, there will always be light for those who are attached to the Source of life.

Moshiach is deeply hidden, but he is coming when we least expect him. He will lead us to a perfect world, a world like Gan Eden, or maybe Gan Eden itself. It will be good, better than good, an eternal Shabbos. We will get there if we hold on to the rope.

# GLOSSARY

*Aharon:* Aaron, the brother of Moses.
*ahavas Yisrael:* love of one's fellow Jew.
*Akeidas Yitzchak:* the binding of Isaac.
*Am Yisrael:* the Jewish People.
*Anshei Knesses Hagedolah:* Men of the Great Assembly (circa 355–273 BCE).
*arba'as haminim:* the Four Species; bundled plants used on the holiday of Sukkos.
*Aron Kodesh:* the Holy Ark in the Temple.
*Avraham Avinu:* our forefather Abraham.
*Avos:* the Patriarchs.
*baal tefillah:* the person who leads the prayer service.
*Bamidbar:* the Biblical book of Numbers.
*Bayis Rishon:* the First Temple.
*Bayis Sheini:* the Second Temple.
*Beis Hamikdash:* the Holy Temple in Jerusalem.
*berachah:* blessing.
*Beraisa:* later-era Tannaic work, written to explain the principles of the Mishnah.
*Bereishis:* the Biblical book of Genesis.
*binah yeseirah:* a greater level of understanding.
*B'nei Yisrael:* the Children of Israel, the Jewish People.
*Bris Bein Habesarim:* the covenant G-d made with Abraham (in Genesis 15).

*Chad Gadya:* a song that is sung at the end of the Passover Haggadah, describing how G-d will slay the Angel of Death.

*Chavah:* Eve, the mother of all mankind.

*chayos:* a group of angels that surround G-d's Throne of Glory.

*Chazal:* the rabbis of the Mishnah and Gemara.

*chessed:* kindness, goodness, or good deeds.

*chevlei Moshiach:* the birth pangs of Moshiach.

*chiddush:* original or unique thought, usually said regarding an explanation of Torah.

*chillul Hashem:* desecration of G-d's Name.

*Chol Hamoed:* the intermediate days of Passover and Sukkos.

*choshuve:* (Yiddish) honorable, usually refers to people of high stature.

*churban:* destruction, particularly referring to the Holy Temple.

*daven:* pray.

*Devarim:* the Biblical book of Deuteronomy.

*Dovid HaMelech:* King David.

*dor haMabul:* the generation of the Flood.

*Eichah:* the Biblical book of Lamentations, written by Jeremiah the prophet.

*Eisav:* Esau, progenitor of the Western nations and Jacob's twin brother.

*eishes chayil:* literally, a "woman of valor," referring to one's wife.

*Eretz Yisrael:* Land of Israel.

*gadol:* a great rabbi.

*galus:* exile.

*Gan Eden:* the Garden of Eden.

*Gehinnom:* Hell.

*Gemara:* the Talmud, explanation of the Mishnah.

*gematria:* the numerical value of Jewish letters and words.

*geulah:* redemption.

*Goliyas:* Goliath.

*Hadran:* the prayer said when one finishes a tractate in the Gemara.

*haftarah:* a passage from the Prophetic writings, read after the Torah reading in the synagogue on Shabbos.

*Haggadah:* a book recounting the Exodus from Egypt, read at the Seder on Pesach.

*Har Habayis:* the Temple Mount.

*Har Sinai:* Mount Sinai.

*Hashem:* G-d.

*Hevel:* Abel, the son of Adam and Eve.

*Imahos:* the Matriarchs.

*kashrus:* the Jewish dietary laws.

*kavyochol:* "So to speak," when attributing human attributes to G-d.

*Kayin:* Cain, the son of Adam and Eve.

*kehunah:* the Priesthood, the descendants of Aaron.

*Keruvim:* golden angelic figures that stood upon the Aron Kodesh.

*Kiddush Levanah:* lit., sanctification of the moon; the monthly blessing praising G-d for creating the moon.

*Klal Yisrael:* the community of the people of Israel; the Jewish nation.

*Kodesh Hakodashim:* the Holy of Holies; the most inner room of the Holy Temple.

*Kohen Gadol:* the High Priest.

*Kosel:* the Western Wall.

*k'rias Yam Suf:* the parting of the Red Sea.

*Luchos:* the two stone tablets on which the Ten Commandments were inscribed.

*Mabul:* the Flood; the great deluge at the time of Noah.

*madreigah:* spiritual level.

*makkah:* plague.

*Makkas Choshech:* the Plague of Darkness.

*Mashgiach:* yeshiva rabbi who provides spiritual guidance.

*midbar:* the desert.

*migdal Bavel:* the Tower of Babel.

*Minchah:* the afternoon prayer service.

*Mishkan:* the Tabernacle built in the desert, precursor of the Holy Temple.

*Mishnah:* the Oral Torah; the basis of the Talmud, explained by the Gemara.

*Mitzrayim:* Biblical Egypt.

*mitzvah:* a Torah commandment; a good deed.

*Moshe Rabbeinu:* Moses.

*Moshiach:* the Messiah.

*Moshiach ben Dovid:* the Messiah, son of David.

*nes:* a miracle.

*nevuah:* prophecy.

*Noach:* Noah.

*nusach:* the uniform or standard expression, as in prayer.

*Ohel Moed:* the Tent of Meeting in the desert Tabernacle.

*pasuk:* a verse in the Torah.

*Pesach:* Passover.

*Ribbono Shel Olam:* Master of the Universe, G-d.

*ruchniyus:* spirituality.

*Satan:* the evil inclination; the Angel of Death.

*Shabbos:* the Sabbath.

*Shacharis:* morning prayer service.

*Shamayim:* Heaven.

*Sanhedrin:* the Supreme Court of seventy-one judges in the time of the Holy Temple.

*Seder:* the Passover night ceremony when the family gathers to recount the story of the Exodus of Egypt and to eat a festive meal together.

*Shechinah:* the Presence of G-d in this world.

*Shemoneh Esreh:* the blessings of the Amidah prayer, which forms the main part of the prayer service.

*Shemos:* the Biblical book of Exodus.

*shlita:* a Hebrew acronym for "May he live for many good days, amen."

*Shlomo HaMelech:* King Solomon.

*shemittah:* the sabbatical year, when the land lies fallow in Israel.

*Shmuel HaNavi:* Samuel the Prophet.

*shtetl:* (Yiddish) Jewish town or village in pre-war Europe.

*shul:* (Yiddish) a synagogue.

*siddur:* a prayer book.

*sinas chinam:* causeless hatred between two Jews.

*talmid:* a student.

*Tanach:* the Written Torah, including the Prophets and the Writings.

*tefillah:* prayer.

*tefillin:* leather boxes encasing specific verses from the Torah, worn by Jewish men on the head and arm during morning prayers.

*teivah:* an ark.

*teshuvah:* repentance.

*tzaddikim:* righteous, holy people.

*tzitzis:* knotted fringes attached to four-cornered garments worn by Jewish males to remind them of G-d and His commandments.

*tochechah:* rebuke.

*tzaraas:* a disease of the skin resembling leprosy; Divine punishment for certain transgressions.

*Vayikra:* the Biblical book of Leviticus.

*Yaakov Avinu:* the Patriarch Jacob.

*Yechezkel HaNavi:* Ezekiel the Prophet.

*Yerushalayim:* Jerusalem.

*yetzer hara:* the evil inclination; the Angel of Death; Satan.

*yetzias Mitzrayim:* the Exodus from Biblical Egypt.

*yiras Shamayim:* fear of Heaven.

*Yirmiyah:* Jeremiah the prophet.

*Yishmael:* Ishmael, father of the Muslims, son of Abraham and Hagar.

*Yitzchak Avinu:* the Patriarch Isaac.

*Yosef:* Joseph, son of the Patriarch Jacob, who became viceroy of Egypt.

*zt"l:* a Hebrew acronym for "*zeicher tzaddik l'vrachah*—may his memory be for a blessing."

# ABOUT THE AUTHOR

Roy Neuberger is the author of *From Central Park to Sinai: How I Found My Jewish Soul* (Jonathan David Publishers, 2000), *Worldstorm* (Israel Bookshop, 2003), *2020 Vision* (Feldheim Publishers, 2008), and *Working Toward Moshiach* (Shepherd Books, 2015). He also writes a weekly column in *Yated Ne'eman*. He and his wife have spoken before hundreds of audiences in fifteen countries.

The author can be contacted at info@2020vision.co.il or through his website at www.2020vision.co.il.